D1246848

SAINT ANGELA

SAINT ANGELA

The Life of
Angela Merici Foundress of the Ursulines
(1474–1540)

BY

PHILIP CARAMAN

FARRAR, STRAUS AND COMPANY
New York

Copyright © 1963 by Philip Caraman
Library of Congress catalog card number 64-14687
First printing, 1964

NIHIL OBSTAT: Joannes M. T. Barton, S.T.O., L.S.S.,
Censor deputatus
IMPRIMATUR: ✠ Georgius L. Craven, Episcopus Sebas-
topolis Vic. Cap. Westmonasterii, die 28ᴬ Junii 1963

Manufactured in the U.S.A.

To

THE URSULINES

Contents

Illustrations

Introductory Note

This book is a biography of St Angela, the sixteenth-century foundress of the Ursulines, not a history of the Order.

It is not difficult to explain how no life of this saint, whose importance in the Counter-Reformation places her at once alongside St Ignatius, the founder of the Society of Jesus, has previously been written in England. The materials for such a book are scanty. There is not a single extant letter, written or dictated by Angela: her first biographer, Gian Battista Nazari, in many ways remains the best, although he wrote no more than twenty years after her death. The sworn testimonies to her life which he obtained from citizens of Brescia who had known her are most valuable, but together they do not amount to more than a few thousand words. Her short *Rule*, her *Counsels* and *Legacy*, dictated to her secretary, are documents of very great value, but they cover merely the last six years of her life. There can be few great ladies of her century that have presented a more stimulating challenge to their biographer.

There is no question of the greatness of Angela as an innovator and foundress. Today she has between thirty and forty thousand followers, enclosed and unenclosed sisters, a larger family group than that of St Francis or St Benedict. Rome has recognized this and has given her statue a place among the principal founders of religious orders in the north transept of St Peter's.

She is, in fact, the first foundress of a religious Order of women in her own right.

This book does not claim to be definitive biography. Probably it leaves out no known fact about Angela herself: but what interest it has derives from the attempt to explain how a simple but carefully nurtured country girl could have such an influence on her times.

Only by visiting the places associated with her was it possible to reach new conclusions. The greater part of the fresh material in this book is therefore topographical in character. The State archives in Brescia and elsewhere have been searched many times in the last hundred years and have yielded nothing new. Here and there a little new ground has been broken and new inquiries at least opened.

It was Mother Angela Mary, Provincial of the English Province of the Ursulines of the Roman Union, who asked me to write the book and made it possible for me to visit all the places associated with St Angela, from Desenzano to Mount Sion. The photographs, with very few exceptions, were taken by Fr Anthony Powell, and are strictly illustrations of the text. I am most grateful to him for his painstaking, patient and expert co-operation.

Several members of the Roman Union have helped me by their criticism to make the book less unworthy of its subject than it might have been.

SAINT ANGELA

1

Desenzano

St Angela's home, two miles outside Desenzano, can be seen today in much the same condition as it was in the fifteenth century. The farm is still worked—a fair-sized property of undulating fertile land, sheltered from Lake Garda by a gentle rise in the hills to the south of it. The hedges and boundaries of the fields are unaltered. The house stands some ten yards back from the road, a long two-storey house typical of the dwellings of well-to-do farmers who live close to their animals. On the right of the entrance path is a well which for centuries provided water for the occupants. The old cow-pen on the right of the porch is still used. Above it is a large open space that serves as a hayrick and store for fruit. Inside, the large rooms have undergone little reconstruction, although the section of the house nearest the road which had fallen into ruin has recently been restored.

At the time of Angela's birth in 1474[1] Grezze, as the house has been called since the time of St Angela to the present day, was then the home of a rich and independent

---

[1] 1474 is the traditional date of Angela's birth and is the date engraved on the base of the statue in the old harbour at Desenzano. The only document that refers directly to her age is the deposition of Pandolfo Nassino (1540): 'On 27 January died Sister Angela, daughter of the late Thomas de Merici of Desenzano, aged between sixty-five and seventy.' (Brescia Bibl. Queriniana. C. I, 15, f. 574.)

farmer. To speak of a humble cottage is misleading. Early writers on St Angela, misled by the present condition of the house, have concluded that she came from humble and peasant stock. There is little to bear this out. In the England of that day Angela's family would have belonged to the lesser gentry which, under the new Tudor monarchy, was seeking wealth, position and nobility in a fluid society. In Spain she would have been a little lower in social standing than the class-conscious Ignatius Loyola. The short authentic accounts of St Angela make it clear that she was always at her ease with people of upbringing; she was unembarrassed and natural when she met the Sforzas and Gonzagas; her first friends were notable ladies of Brescia and other cities of northern Italy. By the standard of her day she was highly educated in behaviour and manners, though not perhaps in letters. There is ample evidence that she was appreciative of art, valued education, and, even as a child, had a knowledge of the world beyond her township and country. While she had the endurance of a country girl, her natural gift of command, her imperturbability and effortless power to attract others, indicate a breeding beyond that of a peasant girl. From the little that is recorded of the Merici family it is certain that it was well established and well esteemed in the district, and owned land, not only outside Desenzano and in the town itself, but towards Salo, at Brudazzo.

Most biographers of Angela state that she was born at Grezze. However, there is a local tradition that has persisted to this day that puts her birthplace in the town

of Desenzano, in the narrow and fashionable steep
street leading from the harbour up to the castle. This
alternative claim is interesting, since it confirms the
standing of the Merici family and shows also a desire of
the people of Desenzano to bring their *santa* nearer home.

Desenzano is the largest and southernmost town on
the west shore of Lake Garda. It lies at the terminal of an
old trade road from Germany that follows the Trento
valley and comes out on the north of the lake at the
town of Torbole, dramatically situated at the base of a
triangular and isolated mountain. From Torbole it
makes its way precipitously down the western bank of
the lake past Riva, Gargnano, Gardone and Salo to
Desenzano, where it forks east to Verona and Venice,
west to Brescia and Milan. Along this route came also
new ideas concerning religion and authority that were
to have so much influence on northern Italy in the lifetime of St Angela.

Apart from the sea front Desenzano has altered little
since the fifteenth century. The long curving bay formed
a calm anchorage without any artificial breakwater.
Behind the lake front the small streets rising steeply to
the castle site are unchanged. The castle itself has gone;
only the surrounding walls stand: the keep has been replaced by untidy slum tenements. But old drawings of
Desenzano indicate that the fortifications followed the
general pattern of the chain of castles on both the east
and west shores of the lake, which varied only in their
dramatic setting and in the girth of the outer ramparts.
A pictorial map of the district of Brescia, drawn in the

year of Angela's birth, shows an outer line of town walls which has disappeared without trace. If Angela was born below the castle and not at Grezze, it was perhaps because the family had sought safety within the town from the intermittent fighting between Venice and the Duchy of Milan.

All the town houses dating from the sixteenth century show Venetian influence in their mullioned windows and in their decorative patios and balconies. The old parish church of St Mary Magdalen, where Angela was christened, exists no longer. When she was a girl of eight it was pulled down and rebuilt on a plan more in keeping with the growing ambitions of the town. This plan, later elaborated by Tedeschini, was never completed. Today the church is a curiosity, with a vast colonnaded transept and no nave. A fine ornate doorway on the east side relieves the deadening effect of a nineteenth-century reconstruction.

Angela's mother came from the township of Salo. She belonged to the prosperous merchant family of Biancosi. Nineteenth-century biographers hint that her mother married below her station, but this is a piece of unnecessary apology, for the Mericis were at least as well-to-do and probably as well born as the Biancosis. The child's fair hair, clear complexion and short stature, recorded by the earliest biographers, set her in a type that is easily recognized on the western shore between Desenzano and Gardone, but is rarer on the Venetian side of the lake, and is hardly known farther east. There is little lost by the lack of records of her childhood days.

What might have been recorded would only have obscured the fact that she was a child of the lake and little different from the other children of Desenzano: gay, affectionate, religious, growing quickly to a sense of responsibility towards her parents and trained in early years to share their work.

A painting in Desenzano church shows Angela as a small child sitting on her father's knee in a field beyond Grezze. Beside her is her mother and a young girl, probably her elder sister or perhaps a cousin from the estate at Brudazzo. It is one of a series of six small canvases by the same painter, Ricci Calcinardi. They have little artistic merit but much interest for the historian, for Calcinardi was an architect rather than an artist and had an exact eye for reproduction of detail in landscape and interior. In this first painting of the series the rising slope across the road from Grezze and the countryside to the north and south of it are precisely drawn—the olive trees, hedges and distant buildings stand where they stand today; every detail has almost photographic precision.

Here also is confirmation of one of the few facts told of Angela's childhood, namely that her father read to her daily from the lives of the saints.

Nineteenth-century hagiographers have laid hold of this as proof that Angela's parents were pious folk and that the child was born into the kind of family which might have been expected to give the world a great saint. There is some truth in this, but more interest lies in the fact that her father possessed what was then a rarity, namely books, and was himself sufficiently educated to read to his wife and daughter. It was a time when there were few books in print, even in the Republic of Venice, the home of Italian printing, and it is not difficult, therefore, to trace the volume held in the hands of Angela's father. No individual lives of saints had yet been published; only a collection entitled *Legenda Sanctorum* by Jacopo de Voragine, translated from the German by Nicolo Manerbi. It was printed in Venice by Janson in 1475, a year after Angela's birth.[1]

It was the same book that was the beginning of St Ignatius's conversion, when, after the bones of his leg had been shattered at Pamplona, he could find nothing better to read during his convalescence at Loyola Castle. For Angela it was her introduction to the story of St Ursula, a saint fittingly given generous space by the German author who dedicated his work to Geson, Archbishop of Cologne. For Vittore Carpaccio and for the Brescian as well as for the Venetian artists in search of new subjects for their paintings, the story of the fourth-century virgin martyr and her eleven thousand companions, told with such detail, drama and royal background, provided an inspiration that endured beyond Angela's lifetime.

The effect of this book on Angela was great. From childhood, and not, as most biographers write, from her middle life, she was acquainted with the story of the

[1] The identification of the book as the *Legenda Sanctorum* is confirmed by a statement recorded in the process of beatification, cf. Bonifacja Werner, *St Angela Merici*.

British princess. The book also explains her mature and very early interest in the martyrs of the first Christian centuries.

The Company of St Ursula was the name she was to give her followers. There can be little doubt that her interest in St Ursula had its beginning on her father's knee. The outline of the story was to gather associations as she travelled through Italy and was to deepen her attachment to the early Christian heroes. Along with this went a lifelong interest in the tombs of the martyrs, which became her favourite places of pilgrimage in the north of Italy and in Rome—not from any romantic desire to live in an age that was past, but for more urgent reasons. The early martyrs were nearest to Our Lord in time, and an attachment to them naturally produced a sense of the continuity of the Church which was threatened by counterfeits from the north.

On the reverse of the old pictorial map of the district of Brescia is a series of country scenes portraying the activity of farmers in the district of Desenzano during the years of Angela's childhood. It is not easy to follow the round of the year's work, but we can distinguish in the faded watercolours the straw-laden wagons drawn by oxen, the baskets filled with eggs and grapes, the hay-harvesting, the *marmotte*, hawks and falcons. The farmers working the Merici estate today point with pride to a small spring, four hundred yards from Grezze, down a track in the maize field, where Angela brought the midday meal to peasant workers employed by her father. The sun was parching. The men had begun to curse because they had nothing to drink. At the first sound of swearing it is said that Angela prayed; at once a spring shot up from the ground to relieve their thirst.

This may well be the first of the legends that the devout have created to compensate for absence of childhood records. It is more valuable as an example of the local interest in the saint of Lake Garda. To this day Angela's name is known to the country people: trees, small tufts of rising ground, hedges and mounds are pointed to by farm workers who know exactly the traditional association of these features with their saint and perhaps can be trusted more than foreign biographers who have never visited the locality.

It is known that Angela had an elder sister, sufficiently close to her in age to share her childhood ambitions and dreams. Some writers say on slender evidence that she had several sisters and brothers. If she did, it is certain that none appears in the story of her later childhood or adult life.[1] Her sister's name is unknown, but she, like Angela, was influenced by their father's reading of *Legenda Sanctorum*, and understandably both resolved to imitate the practices of the saints recorded in that book.

[1] Bellantini, in his *Life* of St Angela (Chapter 10) speaks of a nephew, but he may well have been the child of Angela's cousin. It is difficult to know how much reliance should be placed on the genealogical tree of the Merici, produced by Merico Merici of Darso during the process of beatification in the seventeenth century. This tree shows that Angela had an elder sister and three elder brothers.

While still very young, Angela and her sister began to fast. They hid in the hayrick above the porch to say their prayers. There were no crusades at the time, but as the existence of new worlds came to the knowledge of Europe, the lives of Franciscan missionary priests inspired Angela and her sister with the vision of fresh worlds to conquer for Christ.

Whether as a result of excessive penance or for some other cause, Angela's sister died at Grezze whilst still very young.[1] Their mutual attachment had been intensified by their father's death a short time earlier. Close to her sister in age and deeply affectionate, Angela felt the loss keenly, and was seized with a childish and impatient longing to know whether she was in heaven. In her immaturity she may have been curious also to discover to what extent her pious practices had, so to speak, availed her. But it is at this time that the first authenticated intervention of the supernatural in her life is recorded.

It occurred at a spot some three hundred yards beyond Grezze, probably still within the estate, a place distinctive enough to have its own name—Barchetto.

For many days, with the directness that spiritual writers blame in anyone but a child, Angela had prayed daily to know the supernatural fate of her sister. It was at Barchetto that the answer came. At midday, with the sun shining on Sirmione and the Venetian bank of Garda, she reiterated her petition during the prayer she made

[1] A number of writers state that her sister died later, when Angela was at Salo, but local tradition does not support them.

to distinguish morning from afternoon. In the sky she suddenly saw a troop of angels, and in their midst her sister, happy and triumphant. Angela carried the recollection of this vision with her throughout her life.

Her most intimate family ties, with her father and her sister, shattered in so short a time, were to be compensated in later life by the close bonds that held her own spiritual children together. In the two guiding visions of her life, it is the *familia*, not the individual, that characterizes them.

There is something sternly realistic in such an appealing vision observed unexpectedly in the full glare of the Garda sun by a young country girl; and it is characteristic of the few recorded mystical experiences in Angela's life that each marked a stage in her development. This vision gave her strength to take on the role of young companion and helper to her mother, and later, after her mother's death, to stand alone in the world without parental support. Independence and self-reliance were forced on her at an early age. Later they developed into a serene security of judgement that made her confident in her own ideas and unswayed by the religious fashions of her day.

None of the early biographers of Angela gives the exact dates of the early break-up of her immediate family. Between the ages of twelve and fifteen she was certainly left an orphan.

For a period lasting between five and seven years after the death of her father and sister, she lived alone with her mother in the large house in Grezze, taking increasing responsibility for the farm and home. It was perhaps the time of her most rapid development. We know for certain that when her mother died she was still a child. The house and farm then passed temporarily, it would seem, to relatives, and Angela was sent to Salo, twelve miles north of Desenzano, to live with her maternal uncle.

At Barchetto, the site of her first vision, there stands a small chapel. A group of farm buildings, dating from the early seventeenth century, leads up to it. Above the altar in the chapel there is a painting by Andrea Celesti, who also did a fine series of large canvases on the life of St Mary Magdalen in the parish church of Desenzano. The painting shows the Blessed Virgin enthroned, with the Holy Child on her knee, surrounded by four saints: Angela, Anthony of Padua, Laurence and Philip Neri. It is one of the earliest paintings of the saint after the portraits of Moretto done in the thirty days after her death when her body awaited burial in S. Afra's church in Brescia. The Barchetto picture shows Angela in her middle age, with strong features, high cheekbones, fair complexion and light-coloured hair. She is in the dress of a Franciscan Tertiary, with staff in her left hand and in her right hand a book with the scarcely decipherable legend, *Beata Angela Peregrina*. The Franciscan Rule and constant pilgrimages were to fashion her spirit. Both had their beginnings at Salo. When she moved there from Desenzano her childhood dreamings were over.

2

Girlhood at Salo

No more than half a day's ride north from Desenzano, on the same side of the lake, Salo, even today, differs so much in character from Desenzano that the young Angela, on reaching her uncle's home, must have felt she was arriving in a strange country. Salo also was a Roman town. Some historians put its foundations earlier and derive its name from Saloo, an Etruscan chief who had fled his country during a plague; others say its name comes from an old dialect word meaning exit, for it was an outpost of Roman Italy in the north. Here the lake begins to narrow; its mood is more unsettled and occasionally violent, while in the south it is normally calm. It is at Salo that the mountains, steep but not inaccessible, come down to the lake shore, from the Volciano range, dominated by S. Bartolomeo, which separates Garda from Lake Idro. Farther north the range falls precipitously into the water. In Angela's time the lakeside towns were connected mainly by water.

Set in a small, deep and protected bay, Salo was perhaps the most perfect anchorage for fishermen on the western shore. It had a direct road connection through the hills with Brescia and became prosperous on its catches of trout and carp. Apart from the single strip of buildings along the bay, where hotels and shops have displaced the fishermen's houses, it appears today much the same as it did at the close of the fifteenth century. The small houses, many of them dating from this period or even earlier, run in three narrow parallel streets along the last slope of the hills, from the cathedral at the north end of the town to the Franciscan church at the south—two buildings which would become closely associated with Angela's mature girlhood. Between these streets, with their recessed workshops, are narrow, shaded alleyways. The more prosperous families resided in what is now the Via Gerolamo Fantoni, and the merchants in the Via di Mezzo. The rise on which the town is built is so sharp that long flights of steps lead up from the street entrance to each house through terraced gardens to the main door.

The house occupied by the Biancosis cannot now be identified. It was probably not unlike the house close to the cathedral, in the Via Fantoni, where Charles Borromeo stayed, and perhaps in the same street, for all Angela's biographers insist that the Biancosis were a prosperous family.

This girl of striking beauty, from a strange town, unusually prayerful and serene, and living with one of the principal families of the town, must have attracted attention. Moreover, it was manifest, even at this time, that the child's main interest was with God. From her first days at Salo her prayer and fasting were constant, but there is no suggestion in early biographies that they weakened her constitution. To the end of her life Angela was a tireless and hard rider of exceptional courage, with a capacity to undertake long journeys that would have fatigued many younger people. It is only an examination of her shrunken and entombed body at S. Afra's in Brescia that might seem to give some grounds for the statement that in her childhood she was indiscreet in her practices of penance and that this indiscretion stunted her growth. But it must be remembered that she belonged to a stock of people below average in stature and she was typical of them.

Her uncle and aunt were practical as well as good people. They understood her piety, and at the same time restrained its excessive expression—a lesson that endured and is manifest in the directness and balance of Angela's teaching and, at a time when florid phrasing was the fashion, in the absence of any extravagant expressions in her *Rule*. Moreover it was at Salo that she came across the first and most enduring influence in her spiritual life.

The Franciscans of the Observantine Order had established a house and church at Salo in the fourteenth century. It was totally destroyed by an earthquake in 1910. Indeed, today it is difficult, even from records, to reconstruct its appearance. The present building is on the site of the old church, but bears no resemblance to it.

It was through this church that Angela, like so many of the later medieval saints, came under the formative spiritual influence of the Friars. Her biographers agree that she was drawn to them chiefly because membership of the Third Order gave her the opportunity to receive Holy Communion more frequently and at an earlier age than she could have done at the cathedral at the north end of the town. Although the first Franciscan

Rule prescribed Communion only at the three great feasts of the year, Christmas, Easter and Pentecost, already by the time Angela entered the Order at Salo the feasts of Our Saviour and Our Blessed Lady had been added, as well as the feasts of the Apostles and of all the saints, men and women, of the Order. Angela therefore would have been able to communicate weekly, a very uncommon practice indeed in the sixteenth century, for the Rule encouraged even more frequent approach to the Sacrament 'if the confessor or ghostly Father gave leave'.

The Third Order, besides, offered Angela the guidance of a rule of life. Designed by St Francis 'for all sorts of persons whose desire is to live devoutly in their own houses . . . and to give themselves to the works of piety', it had proved its efficacy in the large number of saintly men and women who had embraced it. Neither at this time nor at any period of her later life does Angela appear to have been drawn to join any of the enclosed Orders of women. The lay branch of the Franciscans, as both she and St Francis saw it, offered the fullness of the religious life without the cloister. As with other orders, the postulant on entering made a general confession covering her lifetime. After admission she was not able to leave the confraternity and return to the world, but was allowed 'free passage' to any other approved Order. Married men or women could enter only with their partner's consent.

Although living at home, members of the Order were distinguished by their dress. They had to wear a 'mean, simple cloth, both in price and colour, neither altogether white nor black', and a large veil of hemp or flax sewn together without plaits; their gowns were to be furred only with lamb, and their purses made of leather without any strings of silk. In the towns in which they lived their conduct was to conform with their simple dress. Banquets and dancing were forbidden. Their day was devoted to prayer, visiting the sick and afflicted; and in all their practices of devotion they were to be governed by their director.

The *Rule* explains Angela's life from her days at Salo till her death: and it explains also one of the few facts that are recorded of Angela in her youth, namely, her constant practice of penance. 'Our Lord has given me the grace,' writes St Francis in his 'Will' which prefaced the *Rule*, 'to begin a life of penance.' From the *Rule* also Angela derived her devotion to the beads which appear in all her portraits, for members of the Order who could not read the Office, were to say fifty-four *Pater Nosters*—twelve for Matins and Lauds and seven for each of the other hours—and after each *Pater Noster* a *Gloria*. There is emphasis also on daily Mass.

Here undoubtedly are the foundations of Angela's spiritual life and here also the beginnings of her Company. Members of the Third Order were to consider themselves called by God to exercise an apostolate in their own families and in the circle in which they moved, in order to make them devout and regular in the service of God. They were urged to give their time to Christian instruction of children, and to concern themselves with the spiritual welfare of the sick and the dying. Pilgrimages were encouraged and exemption from Office granted at such times.

This *Rule*, rather than any director, shaped Angela's life. Only in her middle years, after her spiritual formation was complete, did she come under any strong personal influence.

She was then sufficiently mature to have confidence in her own vocation, and not to be influenced by forceful example into undiscerning imitation.

The story is told, and it belongs to the Salo period of her life, of a childish or rather adolescent episode which illustrates the impact of the *Rule* on her young imagination. Like Ignatius Loyola, Angela had learnt from the *Legenda Sanctorum* about the austerities practised by the saints, not only remote saints of the desert like Anthony and Paul, but others nearer her time and place. She would certainly have heard also of the fame of Nicholas von Flue, whose eremitical life and repute for holiness had come down through the Trento valley to Salo. He had died in 1487 when Angela was thirteen—the father of a family, a soldier, and then a magistrate before he had retired to Mont Jon in the canton of Unterwald, where his cell became a place of pilgrimage for thousands who sought his advice and prayers.

At an age that none of her biographers can specify, she left Salo for the mountains to lead a life of penance on the pattern set by Nicholas von Flue. Her plan was carried out without a word of warning to her uncle. Leaving Salo after Mass, she set out for a grotto in the mountains where she intended to lead a life of prayer unimpeded by her daily household tasks. Possibly she may have had ideas of founding a congregation of women hermits, and the failure of this early fantasy may partly explain her diffidence later in starting her own Order until she could have no possible doubt that it was God's will.

The escape was over in a day. Angela was discovered by her uncle and brought back to Salo.

It is also possible that her flight to the mountains had been suggested to her by the frequent visits she made to the hermitage of St Francis that lay at the entrance to the bay of Salo on the Isola di Garda, that lies off Portese on the spur of land on the opposite side of the bay to Salo, and separated from the tip of the peninsula by a narrow stretch of water no more than two hundred yards long. In 1220 Francis had visited the island and among the ruins of Roman villas had founded a house known as the Romitorio. The house had quickly gathered associations with other saints. Bernardine of Siena, less than fifty years before Angela's birth, had lived for a long time on the northern point of the island, doing penance in a grotto. The little island itself, about three-quarters of a mile in length, was then known as *Frati* or *Zaccolanti* (Recollects) and the Franciscan convent was at the height of its renown. Until well into the sixteenth century it was the resort of saints, poets and savants from all parts of Italy. Here also, apart from gaining spiritual inspiration, Angela would have learnt for the first time to mix with ease, as she did in the large towns of the plain, with painters and persons of distinction.

Her exterior life at Salo followed the pattern of her life at Grezze. She continued to live with her uncle until she was twenty. Her beauty and her physical strength are both mentioned by her earliest biographers, who base their statements on the recollection of men and women who knew her. Young women of her own age were already marrying; and her physical attraction —her fair hair, her poise, the fine bone formation of her face, and the puzzling remoteness of her conduct— must have made her remarkable in the small township. We know that the young men of the town complimented her on her good looks. Moreover, she was due to inherit the house and large property of Grezze.

Angela's life was more retired than that of other girls. She fasted most days, prayed for long hours during the night, and practised forms of penance suggested by her spiritual advisers. On this last point one of her early biographers goes into detail. Basing himself on an early witness he states that she wore a hair shirt. Except when she was under orders from the doctors, she drank wine only at the seasons of Christmas and Easter. Her customary food was bread and vegetables, except in Lent when she fasted with greater severity three days a week, eating only a few chestnuts and some fruit. Another contemporary, Agostino Gallo, in a sworn statement, claimed that Angela told him that during her girlhood she did all the ordinary fatiguing household work done by women, like cooking, baking and drawing water, and that for a week at a time she would eat nothing, except as much bread as could be held in the palm of the hand. And he added that Angela had made a gesture with her left hand over her right, 'to show me the quantity of bread she used to eat'.

Only on one other recorded occasion did Angela speak of her life at this time. It was many years later when she was discussing with Agostino the pride of pseudo-mystics and their fallacious claims to special revelations. To illustrate how easily pious people could be misled, Angela gave this example from her own experience. 'Many years ago,' reports Gallo on this conversation with Angela, 'Satan appeared to her in the form of an angel, and he was so beautiful that no man could believe or imagine such beauty: but God had mercy . . . on her soul and enlightened her so that she suddenly threw herself down on her face and cried, "Get to hell, enemy of the Cross, for I know that I am not worthy to behold any angel of God".'

The manner in which Angela told the story impressed Gallo; for while Angela gave it as an example of a youthful delusion, Gallo took it as an indication of her sanctity that she considered herself unfit for any special favours of heaven. In her own esteem she was a normal child. There was no display in her practices of penance, which were known to none except her relatives and confessor. To the inhabitants of Salo she was as much an object of respect as of love. They admired her life of discipline in an age of loose morals. At this period young ladies of Angela's bent were already in convents of the strictest enclosure. But Angela, like Ignatius Loyola, unknown to herself, was being led to found a new type of religious Order, without enclosure, without distinctive dress, and without any territorial limits other than those of a fast-expanding world.

At the age of twenty Angela returned to Grezze. At Salo she had prepared herself for her life's work.

3

The Vision of Brudazzo

On joining the Third Order of St Francis at Salo, Angela became known as Sister Angela. At home and on her travels she wore the rough, untailored and unbleached woollen garment of the Franciscans, with a white veil on her head. It is in this dress that she is represented in all the portraits of Moretto and later artists. The pilgrim's staff is always in her hand and beads hang from her cincture.

She returned to Grezze independent and mature. The Biancosis, with whom she had spent the years following her mother's death, are not mentioned again in her life, with the exception of her cousin, Bartolomeo. Salo fades from her story, apart from a single reference in a curious document of a later date in which her contemporary, Pope Clement VII, refers to her as Angela of Salo.

At Grezze she took over the management of her parents' property and at the same time travelled about the lake and through the countryside behind it on journeys which combined the marketing of farm produce with the work of Christian instruction.

This was to be her life for the next twenty years or more, and it made her the best-known lady in the district of Garda and Brescia. From now until a few years before her death, travelling was to occupy much of her time, whether she was going on pilgrimage or on errands of peacemaking in a century marked by incessant family feuds and intermittent warfare. From childhood she had been accustomed to hard riding, and from her first days at Salo she was constantly moving across and along the lake in fishermen's craft. The southern, broader and more shallow basin of Garda at Desenzano was seldom rough, but in the north the waters were frequently and suddenly stirred up to storms. As well as any fisherman who earned his livelihood on the lake, she came to know every small harbour on both shores, every shelter provided by the steep mountains on the north-west side, the dangerous shallow waters off the tip of Sirmione, and the narrow neck of the lake off Tempesta, which in bad weather was perilous even for large vessels. She knew most intimately those places where the Franciscans had established churches.

The eastern side of Garda had been under Venetian rule for many years: in Angela's childhood, castle by castle, town by town, the eastern shore and hinterland yielded to Venice. Salo had fallen as early as 1420; Lonato, a market town larger than Desenzano and only a few miles from it, as late as 1516. The fall of Lonato marked the completion of the Venetian conquest of Garda. It was a large and prosperous town, strongly fortified by walls, and it held the mastery of the plain. For many years after Angela's return from Salo, there was still intermittent fighting for the fortress.

The Franciscan house and church at Lonato lay below the slope of the hill on which the town was built, under the shadow of the vast castle. To judge from its dilapidated cloister, now converted into farm tenements, and from the ruined apse of the church, which serves as a communal barn, it must have been one of the most magnificent churches in the district. Today the fine proportions of the ruins and the neglected frescoes on the dome, showing St Clare with the monstrance raised in her hand, driving back the Sarcens from Assisi, and a few faded paintings of other Franciscan saints, are the only indications of its splendid past. The friary was suppressed by Bonaparte when he occupied the castle in the course of his first Italian campaign. It was never re-established.

Some writers suggest that it was here that Angela was received into the Third Order, but this is unlikely, for it would date her reception after her return from Salo. However, it is certain that in her second period at Grezze this church became her spiritual home. The marketing of the produce of Grezze—the eggs, wheat, corn and grapes that we see in the painting on the reverse of the map of Brescia—would have taken her into Lonato as often as into Desenzano. Indeed, Lonato, as a market, was more important than Desenzano and had better communications with the towns of the plain.

Whether at the suggestion of her Franciscan advisers or on her own initiative, Angela gave much of her time to the teaching of catechism. Possibly it was the example of her own parents that made her see its importance, but it is interesting to observe how closely her apostolate was following the same pattern as Ignatius Loyola's.

From the time of his conversion the Basque saint devoted all the hours he had free from study, to catechetical instruction in the streets of the cities where he was educating himself so laboriously. Like Angela, he was gathering helpers around him, and like her was assisting the sick, the dying and the needy. The ideas of both developed slowly. Both, without knowing it, were to start a revolutionary form of religious life, the one for men, the other for women. There is no evidence that they ever met, though constant travelling took them to the same Italian cities about the same time, even to Venice, the Holy Land and Rome, in a work that was similar in aim and inspiration.

We know that Angela visited all the towns on Lake Garda. Frequently she must have crossed to Sirmione, which, from the time of the Emperor Augustus, had never ceased to be a fashionable summer resort for the rich. The little church of S. Pietro, set amid a grove of olive trees and cypresses, about half a mile north of the point where the fine Scaliger castle sits astride the narrow neck of the peninsula, was at this time in the hands of the Franciscans. The frescoes in the apse and chancel, still well preserved, portray an archbishop, St Francis and popular saints of the age. From a point farther north, through the ruined arch of the massive Roman villa on the headland, Angela could see the peninsula of Portese behind which lay Salo, and to the east Lazise, Cisano, Bardolino and the other towns beneath the range of Monte Baldo. From them several of her earliest companions came.

For just over twenty years after her return from Salo, Grezze was her home, and also the starting-point of all her wanderings about the lake. Several women, influenced by her example, appear to have joined in an informal association with her at this period. They came not only from Desenzano, but also from every town on the lakeside: Peschiera, Salo, Sirmione, Padenghe and Lazise. Their life was like hers; and several of them, like her, belonged to the Third Order of St Francis. They were women of some leisure who joined to their domestic duties the work of Christian instruction.

No exact date is given by her biographers for an incident that was to be the most formative in her life. It occurred within this period at a place then known as Brudazzo, a property lying about a mile back from the lake shore and rather more than the same distance north of Desenzano in the direction of Salo. Here there was a farm which, according to some writers, belonged to relatives of the Merici family. Angela frequently visited it, either to supervise the work on the estate or to see her relatives. In a field, hidden from the shore by a conical hill, she had a vision that resembles the vision of Jacob in the book of Genesis. She saw a ladder stretching from the sky to the earth. Down it came angels and maidens in pairs. The maidens sang and the angels accompanied their song with instruments. Then a voice spoke, giving her to understand that she was destined to found a new Order of women that would be as numerous as her heavenly visitors, stretching into the future as far as she could see into the clear midday sky.

The precise spot of the vision is still preserved in local tradition. Formerly it was marked by a chapel which has disappeared without trace, and then later by a tree which has since fallen. But the peasants that farm the land today point to a young ash sapling as the exact place where Angela was kneeling at the time. The artist who depicted the scene in the series of paintings in Desenzano church, though usually most exact in his detail, has allowed himself the licence of showing on the right of the picture a corner of the lake, which, in fact, could be seen only from the summit of the hill below which Angela was praying. If the spot marked by tradition is exact, Angela was looking towards a farm-house, perhaps the home of her relatives, about five hundred yards distant in the direction of Padenghe and Brescia. As will be seen, it was through friends at Padenghe that she was to move to Brescia and there to begin the work that was to end with the formation of her Company.

The vision of Brudazzo is the best-authenticated mystical experience in the life of St Angela. She remembered always the tune sung by the maidens and the message of the voice, though it was several years before she fully understood the implications.

For some time after this vision Angela's life remained unaltered. As she became better known she was more sought after at home and perhaps devoted less time to travelling. At Grezze she was visited by many families from as far away as Brescia and often gave them hospitality. She was received by them in return when they passed the summer months in their villas on Lake Garda.

It is not known when Angela first met Caterina, the widow of Gian Battista Patengola, a rich citizen of Brescia. The family owned a summer residence at Padenghe, in a bay of Lake Garda about three miles north of Desenzano. The village, now half a mile inland, then lay on the shore and above it a number of well-built houses climbed the steep hill on which the Scaligers had built another impressive fortress. Like the castle at Lonato, it had recently seen fighting between the Milanese and the invading armies of France.

At this time Caterina Patengola had lost two sons and in her distress sought out Angela for comfort during one of her visits to Padenghe.[1] In 1516 she persuaded Angela to visit Brescia and stay with her there. Through Caterina, Angela met many notable citizens and was able to see for herself that here lay her chance of gathering around her a compact company of ladies who shared her aspirations. In her decision to move from Desenzano to Brescia there is no proof that Angela was directly influenced by her vision at Brudazzo. What finally decided her was not the persuasive arguments of Caterina, but the advice of her Franciscan director whom, by a rule, she was committed to follow. Moreover, she was now a little over forty and she may well have thought it unlikely that she would be able to sustain for much longer the continual journeyings in all weathers from one lake town to another, though, in fact, some of her most wearisome pilgrimages lay ahead.

[1] cf. The deposition of Antonio Romano.

Such hesitation as she showed was due in part to her reluctance to lead a more public life. On her first brief visit to Brescia, which lasted six months, she lodged without privacy in the house of Caterina Patengola. There she met Antonio Romano, who offered her rooms in his own house where she would be free to follow her chosen way of life with the same independence that she had known at Grezze. Antonio himself tells of her coming to live with him. 'About the year 1517,' he says, 'I went a number of times to the house of Donna Caterina, widow of Don Giovanni Battista di Patengola, and there staying in her house was Sister Angela from Desenzano, who belonged to the Third Order of St Francis. She had come to comfort Donna Caterina after the death of her two sons. Each time I went Sister Angela grew to like me more and eventually she arranged to come and lodge in my home.' It was there that Angela, for the next fourteen years, came to have her own apartment in Antonio's house adjoining the church of St Agatha.

4

First Years at Brescia

Antonio Romano lived in the very centre of Brescia, in the narrow Via S. Agata, a short street connecting the two principal market-places of the city. There are only a few buildings in this street, and it is probable that Romano's home adjoined St Agatha's, a fine newly constructed house set back a little from the road through a low, arched entrance. Like other houses in the same street, it had an exterior staircase leading up from a shaded courtyard to balconies connecting the rooms on all four floors. It was large enough to give Angela the privacy she sought. Its central position also was an advantage to her in her work.

Henceforth Angela's life and the life of her followers was to be spent in towns. And it was in towns also that all the houses of her Company were to be established throughout Europe and New France.

During Angela's childhood and early womanhood Brescia, which now became the city of her adoption, had been the prize of warring armies of France, Venice and the Empire. When she was a child of nine the Venetian army had finally captured the city from the Milanese after a struggle lasting fifty years, fought along Lake Garda and in the plain south and west of Desenzano. The peace that followed was only a respite. Angela had hardly established herself at Grezze on her return from Salo when in 1494 war broke out once more, this time between Germany and France. The battleground again was northern Italy, and Brescia had little peace. Historians record that the unfortunate city changed hands twelve times during Angela's last seven years at Desenzano. She was there when Charles VIII of France first conquered Brescia, and soon after she watched the retreat of his armies over the Alps as the peal of bells from the campanile of the parish church at Desenzano rang out to speed him on his way. When later Louis XII seized Milan, the Venetians withdrew from Brescia without offering a fight, but they quickly returned in 1512 when the French were again defeated.

As a result of this constant warfare, the leading families of Brescia were bitterly divided in their loyalties. Reprisals, plunder and executions in the cathedral square had followed each change in the city's overlords; and although now it was slowly regaining its prosperity, it was still a distressed and sometimes a famished city. Caterina herself had suffered harshly and experienced little difficulty in persuading Angela that she would have greater opportunity to practise her works of charity in the provincial capital than in the small outlying towns of Garda. Moreover, after such prolonged fighting, there were many widowed ladies, like Caterina herself, who would join her in Brescia and assist her in her apostolate.

Already Angela from her childhood was familiar with the savagery of war and with the plundering habits and guttural speech of the northern mercenaries, who seized all they could from the land over which they fought and brought with them strange doctrines that threatened the faith of peasants and townsfolk alike. However, this association of heresy with foreign armies helped the Italian cities to cherish their faith as a native heritage which no foreign soldiers could take from them.

During the years of fighting, when many of the poorer citizens had fled to the hills and castles for security, Caterina Patengola had lived for the greater part of the year at Padenghe, within an hour's ride of Angela's home at Grezze. Caterina had introduced Angela to the devastation and suffering of Brescia. Together they had made frequent visits to the city, and it is likely that Angela began an occasional mission of mercy there before she finally decided to leave her home and farm and accept Caterina's insistent call to relieve the condition of the citizens. For some time, however, Angela appears to have had some misgivings in accepting without advice Caterina's invitation. From what we know of her, Caterina seems to have been a possessive woman. As she had recently lost her two sons, she treated Angela as her own child. This would explain why in the first place Angela agreed to come to Brescia only for a period of six months, and why she afterwards accepted the offer of Antonio Romano to live privately in his house, where she would have the freedom she needed for her work.

By settling at Brescia Angela was not transferring her political loyalty. The city ruled over a stretch of territory nearly a hundred miles in length. Its eastern boundary took in both Salo and Desenzano. On the north the foothills of the Alps came down to the fringe of the town and their last spur provided an almost unassailable position for the castle. Indeed, the city could be taken only if the walls to the south were first breached. The map of Brescia which marks the castle and walls shows clearly the five rivers that flowed through the plain outside the city and joined the Po to the south. On the west side were the Oglio and Mella; on the east the Naviglio and Chiese; through the very centre flowed the River Garza; until in the fourteenth century it was diverted round the western wall to form a further line of defence. The map also shows the properties of the big families of Brescia and all the areas which they governed.

In Angela's time many towers stood inside the city— the personal fortresses of warring noble families. Angela's mission was one of peacemaking among them. As her work met with success, these family towers became purposeless and, soon left tenantless, fell into ruins. For guidance in her mission, she took the Chapter in the Franciscan Rule that gave her instructions for handling quarrels arising both between 'brothers and sisters' and between 'strangers'. St Francis's own earlier life had involved him in feuds between his native Assisi and Perugia, and in his *Rule* he wrote from his own hard experience.

Caterina Patengola and Antonio Romano were on terms of equality, if not always on terms of intimacy, with the leading families in the city, and Angela was to make use of her status as Antonio's guest to further her own apostolate. She quickly earned a reputation as the great peacemaker of Brescia. In major disputes she worked under the direction of the bishop, for the *Rule* enjoined that he was to be consulted before an attempt was made at reconciliation.

Among the most important families in Brescia was that of Martinengo. They owned in the plain many hamlets and manors that are marked with the letter *M* on the 1475 map of Brescia. The head of the family was Francesco, a young swashbuckler who roved the streets with his retainers seeking out his principal rival, Filippo da Sala. The night battles between the two factions made the city unsafe for the inhabitants. The intervention of the Podesta, as the Venetian Governor of Brescia was called, was invoked, but without success. Then Angela's help was sought by the womenfolk of the two families. She visited both Francesco and Filippo in their homes and persuaded them to meet each other in her apartment at Antonio's house. This they did, and peace was made. Chiara Martinengo later joined her Company, but her brother Giorgio, handsome, red-haired, well read, *Il Superbo Italiano* as he was called, fell fighting in the cathedral piazza with thirty wounds in his body and a Greek epigram on his lips. This was in a later feud with the family of Avogadro, among whom Angela had many friends.

As her work grew she came to be known in all the province and frequently rode to the outlying dependencies of the Brescian families. In Brescia itself she came to be adopted as a child of the city with the same simple affection that the people of Lake Garda had shown her. Then inevitably her reputation spread to other cities. Before long she was to travel all through north Italy and to the courts of the Gonzagas and of the Sforzas on her apostolate of peacemaking.

For the present, until she gathered a group of companions about her, Romano's house gave her all the facilities she needed for her work. Her biographers do not attempt to give any reason for her constant change of dwelling-place, and the reader is left with the impression of restless activity. But, in fact, each change, as will be seen, corresponded with a development in her apostolate.

Although from the time she was twenty Angela had never ceased travelling, her first recorded pilgrimage was made in 1524 to the tomb of Blessed Osanna Andreasi in Mantua. Osanna was a well-known mystic. Unlike Angela, she had left no congregation behind her to carry on her work. In her childhood she had joined the Third Order of St Dominic and had lived and died in that Order. After her death she came to be adopted as the patron of Mantua by her fellow citizens much in the same way that Angela herself, within a few years of her own death, was to become the saint of Brescia.

It was twenty years after Osanna's death that Angela visited Mantua. Osanna had been beatified ten years previously, for on 8 June 1514 a Brief of Pope Leo X had allowed the clergy of the city to celebrate her Office and Mass as for the feast of a virgin. This limited cult had been granted at the request of her friend,

Isabella d'Este, to whose children she had acted as governess for a number of years. Angela may well have gone to Mantua for the celebration of her feast on 18 June and visited the church of the Poor Clares of S. Lucia where her incorrupt body was venerated.[1]

It is possible that Osanna's high reputation for sanctity in the spirit of the Dominican Rule made Angela hold back from starting her own order. It is mainly in the personal influence they both attained in their own cities that the lives of the two saints were alike. Osanna was well born and well connected, and her parents' house, the Palazzo Valente, opposite the church of S. Aegidio, was one of the finer houses in Mantua.[2] Essentially she was a mystic, while Angela, though not without mystical experiences, might be called a saint of action. When she was no more than five years old, Osanna was granted her first vision. Thereafter she experienced frequent and prolonged ecstasies and also the mystical espousals; and for the last part of her life she bore the sacred stigmata on her body. The events in her life that chiefly impressed her contemporaries are portrayed in relief carvings of beaten gold that decorate

---

[1] Blessed Osanna Andreasi's tomb is now in Mantua Cathedral in a shrine below the altar on the north side. Here her incorrupt body, taller than Angela's and clothed in the habit of the Third Order of St Dominic, can be seen when the casing in front of the altar is removed. On the fingers of the right hand are three rings and there is a crown of roses on her head.

[2] This house, 9 Via XX Settembre, still stands and is used by Dominican Tertiaries.

her tomb. Here in the principal panel she is seen kneeling at the feet of Our Lord, who is revealing his Heart to her; in the second, she is clasping a crucifix in ecstasy; in the third, she is receiving Holy Communion from an angel; and in the remaining two she is shown working among the sick in hospital, and, in a composition similar to the Desenzano picture, standing in the poop of a ship holding a crucifix over the stormy waves.

But Osanna was a prophetess who bewailed the state of her country rather than a saint of action. In the central attachment of her life, namely, the Child Jesus, she was more Franciscan than Dominican, and it was perhaps this that attracted Angela to her. It was as an infant that Our Lord first appeared to Osanna, and thereafter she was never long without some visitation. Her visions were different in character from any that Angela experienced, for when she was a child an angel had led her by the hand to paradise and showed her the divine glory, with the warning: 'Dear daughter, this blessed life cannot be possessed except through true love and holy charity.' A comparison of these words with the words Angela heard at Brudazzo: 'Persevere as you have begun and you shall assure your happiness', summarizes the difference between the two saints.

From Mantua Angela made her way back to Brescia through Solferino in order to visit Prince Luigi Alessandro Gonzaga. Antonio Romano, who may well have been with Angela on this journey, says that the purpose of the visit was to ask the prince's mercy for one of her relatives who had been condemned to exile and the confiscation of his property. Romano adds that Angela was well received by Prince Luigi, who already knew of her work in Brescia. He granted her petition and in turn begged Angela to stay on in his dominions and restore peace amongst its warring factions. Antonio gives no further details. At the time he wrote, Angela was dead and Luigi an old man.

Prince Luigi would have spoken much about Osanna, for Osanna's mother, Agnese Gonzaga, was his cousin. Moreover, Isabella d'Este, Osanna's close friend, had married another Gonzaga. The connections were manifold. Indeed, when Angela was a child at Salo, Isabella had made a pleasure tour of Lake Garda with her children, and had stayed with persons of influence with whom Angela was already in touch. On this tour she had been accompanied by a large retinue of gentlewomen. There had been speeches in her honour and a procession of boats on the lake. It was an occasion for pageantry and feasting such as Garda had never seen before. Possibly on this occasion the lives of Osanna and Angela had crossed momentarily, but this is not recorded.

When Prince Luigi asked Angela to stay on at Solferino he saw in her another Osanna. It was the peculiar genius of the Gonzagas that they combined shrewdness of this kind with political banditry. It is difficult to imagine two more contrasted characters than Prince Luigi Alessandro and Angela. Luigi, the son of Rodolfo, the prince of the Holy Roman Empire who had beheaded his first wife, was a fierce but genial ruffian. His long lifetime was spent in fighting, and he was most famous for his single-handed combats in the jousting field. Three years before Angela's visit he had injured both his eye and leg in battle against the French, and got the nickname, 'Limper-Squinter'. He had all the fierce Gonzaga temperament and at the same time he loved his people and saw in Angela the means of restoring the damage of war, which was his unceasing preoccupation. His motto and boast was inscribed above the entrance to his palace: 'My strength is in my people's love and in the respect of men that are mightier.' Such an inscription helps to fill in the detail lacking in Antonio's account of Angela's visit.

To the last decade of her life Angela guided others, while she herself was constantly searching for guidance. At Mantua at the shrine of Blessed Osanna she received none. Her constant quest was for a definition of the task assigned to her at Brudazzo. While the Franciscan Rule had given her the first impulse in her work, now in the larger world of Brescia, and among her expanding connections with the great families of northern Italy, she was looking for an answer to the problem: in what manner precisely did God wish her to accomplish this task? With this in the forefront of her mind, she set out for the Holy Land in the following year.

5

Journey to Jerusalem

St Angela's visit to the Holy Land is more than an interlude in her life. It is important to see it as part of her progress towards the foundation of her Company. Her motive, like the motive of all devout pilgrims of her time, was penance and a search for an indication of the will of God.

From the foundation of medieval Europe and earlier, a pilgrimage to Jerusalem was the greatest act of devotion a Christian could perform. Neither on the journey nor in the Holy Land itself did a day pass when pilgrims did not face the kind of dangers which St Paul enumerates: shipwreck, brigands, robbery and pirates. All this and more the pilgrims were ready to accept in order that they might follow literally in the footsteps of Our Lord. It was the frame of mind inculcated by all writers on Palestine, particularly by the Franciscans. Friar Felix Fabri, for instance, wrote: *Abiit vagus in via sua. Qui peregrinatur ut evagetur, vitiosus est. Non autem qui evagatur ut peregrinatur.* 'The wanderer goes as his heart suggests. The pilgrim who is determined to wander is sinful, not the wanderer who is determined to go on pilgrimage.'[1]

It was with a sense of privilege and without fear of hardship that Angela set out. Dominican and Franciscan

[1] *Fratris Felici Fabri Evagatorium in Terrae Sanctæ peregrinationem.* (Reprinted Stuttgart, 1843.)

writers on the Holy Places had castigated pilgrims who became faint-hearted and who had second thoughts on reaching Venice, the customary and most convenient port of embarkation: 'There are some who at the mere sight of the sea change their minds, or turn back half-way finding they are unequal to the hardships of the journey.'[1] This is advice echoed perhaps in the *Exercises* of St Ignatius, who set out for Jerusalem twelve months before Angela, in his meditation on the Three Classes of Men. To judge from contemporary writing, a pil-grimage to Jerusalem was a vocation within a vocation. It was a climax of a life of devotion and a proof of sincerity in the following of Christ. Pilgrims started with the resolve, should it be the will of God, to leave for ever relatives, friends, home and brothers, sacrificing all personal comfort, in order to take up the pilgrim's cross.

St Francis had devoted a chapter in his *Rule* to those who wished 'to go to the Saracens'. For him and for many saints that followed, the recovery of the Holy Places was more than a devout dream; it was symbolic of the return of Christendom to its centre. Like both Francis and Ignatius, Angela considered passing the rest of her life in Jerusalem, converting the heathen by a manifestation of Christ's charity.

Antonio Romano, Angela's host and patron, first suggested the pilgrimage to Angela. In his written state-ment he declared: 'For many years I desired to visit the Holy Land. When I confessed the idea to the Venerable

[1] *Fratris Felici Fabri Evagatorium.*

41

Mother Angela, she urgently begged me to take her with me, for she had a burning desire to visit the holy places at Jerusalem.' With Angela and Antonio went Bartolomeo Biancosi, Angela's cousin from Salo, probably at her persuasion.

The assembly point for pilgrims was Venice, which held a monopoly in pilgrim traffic. The possessions of the Republic of Venice in the Adriatic and eastern Mediterranean, including the island of Crete, gave protection to her ships for the greater part of the voyage to Palestine; but at the same time the wealth of her empire made them the prey of pirates.

The pilgrimage of 1524 was due to sail from Venice on the day following Corpus Christi, 26 May. Angela and her friends were ready to leave Brescia when news came that the pilgrimage had been cancelled. Angela and Bartolomeo remained at home. Antonio, as he relates himself, 'left Brescia with the intention of going to the fair at Lanzano, but passing through Venice [he] saw the standard of the pilgrim ships flying, and instantly informed Sister Angela, who came to Venice immediately with her cousin Bartolomeo Biancosi of Salo'.[1]

Angela had only a few days in which to reach Venice.

---

[1] The captains of the pilgrim ships flew their flag on the masts outside the west door of St Mark's. Below the flag stood servants of the rival captains, each touting for passengers and offering either a speedier voyage or better rates or greater comfort. Owing to the alarms of war there appears to have been only one vessel sailing this year.

The direct road took her through Lonato to Desenzano and Peschiera, and beyond Lake Garda through the small villages on the road to Verona, not more than two days' riding from Brescia. It was still country she knew from her childhood, at least as far as Verona, although there is no record of her visiting the city until May 1524, when she entered through the steeply arched bridge, protected by the great tower of the greatest of all the Scaliger castles. Her love for the early martyrs may have directed her to Mass in the old church of St Anastasia, with its frescoed porch and gothic brickwork tower, barely a hundred yards from the Piazza dell' Erbe, the old Roman forum used now as the principal market-place. It was in the very centre of the city, and presided over by the Madonna di Verona, formerly a Roman statue of great majesty. In her haste she is unlikely to have stayed more than a night there. The road to Venice took her out through the Porta Vescova, completed four years before Angela's visit as part of a stronger and wider circuit of fortifications.

About two-thirds of the way between Verona and Vicenza, twenty miles farther on, Angela came to the village of Montebello, set like S. Martino, Caldiero and S. Bonifacio and all the attractive villages along the road, at the foot of the slopes of the Monti Lessini. At the eastern extremity of Montebello flowed the River Chiampo. In the middle of summer it is a dry bed of stones. Only the strength of the present embankment, between twenty and thirty feet high, indicates the force of the stream in spring. (The people of Montebello call it a *casada*.) In May it was in spate and as Angela approached, it appeared an insuperable barrier on her path to Venice. The only crossing was provided by a rough bridge of logs laid insecurely on rocks, perilous even for a sure-footed man. Bartolomeo drove his horse into the stream and crossed safely. Angela's horse reared and refused to breast the water. Her only hope was to risk the bridge. With astonishing courage she set her horse on the first span of logs, and rode it slowly and perilously across. This incident forms the subject of a well-known painting by Facchino. It shows Angela dressed in the riding clothes of her time, a long black dress with flowing sleeves, sitting side-saddle, her head raised in prayer, holding loosely the reins of her grey horse as it nervously picks its steps over the first span of the bridge.

Angela arrived in Venice in time for the feast of Corpus Christi. Fortunately Antonio, while he awaited Angela's arrival, had been able to purchase all the necessities for the journey—food, pillows, mattresses, cushions, as well as barrels of wine, cheese and eggs. None of these articles was provided by the sea captains, who contracted merely for the passage. All guide-books contained lists of requisites and recommendations: most suggested a bright red wine from Padua and a crate containing half a dozen live chickens. Some syrup of ginger was bought as a protection against the great heat the pilgrims would encounter.

While they waited there was much to keep pilgrims occupied. For more than a hundred years the city had been famous for its numerous processions, but in splendour there was none that surpassed that of Corpus Christi, which was always given special poignancy by the solemn leave-taking of the pilgrims which concluded the ceremonies. Gentile Bellini painted the scene in the year 1496. The Doge in tiara and mantle, the foreign ambassadors, the Venetian gentlemen in cloth of gold, crimson velvet, damask and scarlet, and the Council of Ten are seen about to join the procession from the ducal palace on the right of the basilica. The square is depicted exactly as it appeared in Angela's time: the vaulted portals of the basilica still decorated with byzantine mosaics which were shortly afterwards replaced by Titian's work.

The Patriarch carried the Blessed Sacrament. Before him went the schools and confraternities, who sang Eucharistic hymns, and with them the guilds of Venice, the children, scattering rose-petals and flowers from silver bowls; behind, the bishops, abbots, clergy and Senate. The pilgrims about to embark for the Holy Land were assigned a special place. A member of the Senate, aided by a group of officials called the Tolmazzi, was annually appointed to take care of them, interpret for them, provide them with lodgings and see that they were furnished with all they needed for the journey. This year the Senator was Aloysio Guistinano. Angela is unlikely to have made more than a passing acquaintance-ship with him, or to have stayed long enough in Venice to have learned about the people's devotion to St Ursula. This was to come on her return visit.

It was at Venice that the story of St Ursula was better known and more popular than in any other city in Italy. Nine years before Angela's visit, on 8 September 1515, in another procession, the Bishop of Brescia, Paolo Zane, known personally to Angela, had carried the head of St Ursula round the square, and was followed by tableaux representing her life. Even for Venice it was perhaps one of the most splendid processions ever seen. Here, if not on her outward journey, then certainly on her return, the story of St Ursula made an enduring impression on her.

Angela embarked on the eve of Corpus Christi and set sail the following day. As Antonio relates, Aloysio Guistinano, the Senator, accompanied the party as far as their ship, which was probably one of the galleys that customarily made the voyage, a vessel with three banks of oars, constructed of hard timber and fastened by chains, joints and iron clasps. The prow, sixty feet in length and no more than fourteen feet wide, had its own sail above the master's cabin. It was depicted with precision by the artist of Desenzano in the series of paintings in the church there. The painting shows a structure on the poop, a *castellum* with three decks, on the top of which St Angela is standing. On this deck lived the steersman, on the second deck the captain, and on the lowest, distinguished women travellers. Near the mainmast there were seven steps that led down into the pilgrims' quarters, which stretched the full length and width of the ship. To each pilgrim was allotted a pallet with its head against the bulwarks of the ship. Down the central gangway were placed their chests and bags. It was a crude arrangement that gave no protection against rats and vermin.

At sunrise every day a whistle from the *castellum* summoned the pilgrims to prayer. At eight o'clock at another signal they gathered before the mast, facing a crucifix, to recite the prayers of the Mass as far as the Canon—it was never at this time considered safe to offer Mass at sea—and then, omitting the Canon, they continued from the Communion prayer to the Last Gospel. On Sunday these prayers were sung to mark off this day from the rest of the week. At sunset the *Salve Regina* was intoned and taken up by all the pilgrims.

Antonio Romano states that the galley in which he and Angela sailed was unmolested by Turks or by pirates. In the early part of the voyage protection was given by the numerous Venetian colonies in the Adriatic. Ragusa was the strongest point in this chain of possessions, but farther south the Turks had captured and fortified Durazzo, and below Durazzo, the island of Corfu.

Felix Fabri has left a description of life in a pilgrim galley. 'Some sing songs or pass their time with lutes, flutes, bagpipes, clavichords, zithers and other musical instruments. Others discuss worldly matters, read books or pray with beads; others sit still and meditate or pass almost the whole time asleep in their berths; others sit and look at the sea and land and write about them.'

For the most part the galley was propelled by sails,

if the wind was sufficient, and oars were used only on entering and leaving harbour. Between Corfu and Crete storms were frequently encountered and it was customary to spend several days in Candia, the main Venetian base at Crete, for rest and re-equipment. The town and harbour entrance were strongly fortified, and there were many hostels and houses of rich merchants which took in wearied travellers. Within the city walls the spiritual needs of the pilgrims were met by the Franciscans and other clergy from Venice, whose work it was to attend to them.

Either in Crete or between Corfu and Crete, Angela lost the sight of her eyes. Her own account of the incident was given later to Agostino Gallo. 'Angela,' he says, 'was travelling to Jerusalem when she lost her sight. However, as she told me, when she was led to places that stirred her greatest devotion, she saw these places with the eyes of her soul as if she had seen them with her bodily eyes.' Gallo's account suggests complete blindness, but Antonio, who was with her and is the more reliable witness, says that the loss of her sight was 'almost complete'. It is regrettable that Antonio gives no further details. It is only later biographers who give more graphic accounts of the incident, but they appear unsupported by evidence. For instance, there is a story that she was standing on deck and had sighted the harbour at Candia when she was struck stone-blind. Another biographer says this occurred as she was praying before a crucifix in a certain church on the island and that it was before the same crucifix on the return journey that her sight was restored.[1] Two facts only can be established with certainty: that she lost her sight before reaching the Holy Land, and that she saw nothing of the Holy Places. The trial may have been supernatural; on the other hand, it may have been the effect of a hard sea passage joined with the glare of the sun off the waters; but this is unlikely, since eventually her sight was completely restored, and apparently in an instant, before she was back in Venice.

Pilgrim ships normally approached the coast of Acre, and put in there. Beyond the port rose the foothills of Lebanon and the holy mountain of Elias, and Mount Modin with the alleged tomb of the Maccabees. From Acre they sailed down the coast to Jaffa, where the pilgrims landed.

[1] This crucifix cannot now be traced. The old Venetian church, later taken over by the Orthodox and now converted into a museum, is S. Marco, opposite the fountain in the main square at the top of the road leading up from the harbour. If this account of Angela's blindness is true, the incident would have occurred here.

6

The City of David

It was six days before the pilgrims could start on their
journey from Jaffa to Jerusalem. A safe conduct was
needed from the Sultan at Jerusalem. Meanwhile they
remained in the galley, not close inshore, for the water
in the artificial harbour was too shallow for ships of
draught, but some distance out beyond what were
known as Andromeda's Rocks. From here they watched
with curiosity the behaviour of the Saracens on the
shore. Frequently in the evening twenty or thirty inhabitants would ride on camels up and down the sands,
peering in the direction of their ship.

On the return of the messenger in company with the
Guardian carrying the safe conduct, the pilgrims disem-
barked and registered their own and their fathers' names
with a Saracen official. Not even the most distinguished
members of the party were permitted to carry swords,
but had to leave them on board: all, however, were
allowed to hire mules or donkeys, usually at an exorbi-
tant price. Then with the Father Guardian leading them
they set out on the first stretch of their journey, passing
the first night thirteen or fifteen miles from Jaffa, either
at Lydda or Ramleh.

This was the easiest and most attractive part of the
journey. The road went through fertile country covered
with palm trees, orange groves and pomegranates.
'Blossom on blossom,' Isaias had written about this

valley, 'it will rejoice for ever, filling the desert with gladness.' There was no shelter for brigands in this country nor was there any danger of thirst.

The Guardian prepared the pilgrims for their entry into the Holy City by recalling the scriptural associations of the places through which they passed. This tradition had been established by the Franciscans early in the fourteenth century, and it was not unlike the manner in which the pilgrims to Canterbury relieved the weariness of their journey by tales intended to edify the company. Jaffa was the home of Simon the Tanner, with whom St Peter had lodged, and whose house near the port was shown to pilgrims: here also Jonah had embarked for Tarshish. At Lydda, Peter, preaching after the Resurrection, had worked the cure of Aeneas which had led to the conversion of the entire population of the town.

From Lydda, where Angela would have visited the crypt tomb of St George, it was three days' journey to Jerusalem. Two hours' ride beyond the town the road left the valley and began to climb the mountainous country of Judaea through which Our Lady had made her journey to her cousin Elisabeth. Then it became increasingly difficult until it reached the summit of Mount Silo, the *jubilum peregrinorum* that gave pilgrims their first sight of Jerusalem. This was also the last halt before they entered the city through the Jaffa gate. There they were met by two friars carrying a cross, and Angela, leaving the rest of the party, made her way to Mount Sion.

The pilgrims would have reached Jerusalem early in

July, since the journey from Venice usually took between thirty and forty days, and there had been no incident to delay them. The convent for twelve friars had been established on Mount Sion in 1335 when Robert of Naples had regained possession of Jerusalem; and about the same time a guest-house for pilgrims had been built adjoining the convent. Here Angela stayed—a fact recorded in the chronicle of the Franciscan Friar, Giovanni di Calaona, published in Venice a hundred years after Angela's death. 'The servant of God, called Sister Angela of Desenzano,' he writes, 'at that time honoured with her presence the convent of Tertiaries on Mount Sion in Jerusalem.'[1] It was the custom of Tertiaries during the period of their stay to work for their maintenance, and this presumably Angela did. Throughout her visit she wore the habit of the Order and was able in this way to move about the city with less danger to herself. Indeed, as another Franciscan writer of this time pointed out, the Tertiaries were greatly respected by the Saracens, who had regard for the simple dress of the Franciscans, so closely resembling their own, and for their spirit of prayer and penance. Nevertheless, pilgrims were warned not to visit the Holy Places alone, for there was always danger that the unaccompanied Christian would be assassinated. The memory of Ignatius Loyola's visit was still fresh among the Franciscan Fathers, who would have recalled, as they looked down across the city, over Kedron to the Mount of Olives, the anxiety he had

[1] Giovanni di Calaona, *Historia Cronologica della Provincia di Syrie e Terra Santa di Gerusaleme* (Venice, 1649).

The Merici Family. A painting in Desenzano Church

Picture of Angela's vision. Lake Garda is on the right

The Franciscan
church on Sirmione
where Angela used
to pray

Jerusalem

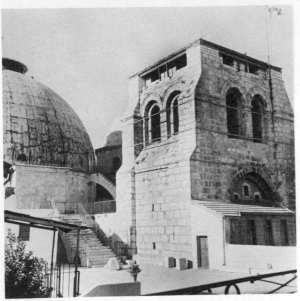

Roof of the church of the Holy Sepulchre

Calvary

Cloister of the Franciscan hostel on Mount Sion where Angela stayed

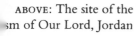

ABOVE: The site of the
sm of Our Lord, Jordan

len of Olives looking
towards Jerusalem

Via Dolorosa, Varallo

Varallo Sesia—S. Monte
Cap.n 36; Gesù e la Veronica (particolare)

ABOVE: Angela on her sick bed at Cremona

L·A·B·ĀGELA·BRISCIANA·VERGINE·FONDATRICE·DELLA·NOVA CGREGATIŌE·DE·VERGINI·DETTA·LA·COPAGNIA·DI·S·ORAOLA·

Angela with her first companions

Die heilige Angela Merici von Defentiano,
Stifterinn der Gefellfchaft der heiligen Urfula;
ihr Leib wird zu Brefcia aufbewahrt in der
Kirche der heiligen Afra bei den Chorherren vom
Lateran; fie ift geftorben *1540* den *27* Jenner.

Old print of Angela as a pilgrim

caused them when on the last day of his pilgrimage, just twelve months before Angela's visit, he had broken from his party and gone out of Jerusalem alone to Mount Olivet, anxious to ascertain the direction in which the alleged imprint of Our Lord's feet was pointing. 'Those who go about without a guide,' wrote Ignatius, wise after the event, 'are in great danger.'

Now on the Mount of Olives the old church of the Ascension was in ruins; in its place had been built a mosque. For while the Moslems rejected the Crucifixion they honoured the mystery of the Ascension. Without any pretence of historical evidence, they believed that God had substituted on the Cross another man in the place of Christ, who had never died and risen again. Like Christ, the great prophet had been taken up to heaven at the end of his life. He would return again on the last day to complete the conversion of all races to Islam.

Cartographers of the day placed Jerusalem at the very centre of the world, and the Cenacle in the centre of Jerusalem. The belief was grounded on a misinterpretation of a mistranslation in the psalm—*Jerusalem circuito eius*. In Christian devotion the Cenacle adjoining the Franciscan convent was the central shrine of the world, for it was associated with three great Christian mysteries: the institution of the Eucharist, the appearance of Our Lord to the Apostles after the Resurrection, and the coming of the Holy Ghost. It is unlikely that Angela was able to visit the building which the Crusaders had converted into a church, since five years before her visit Suleiman the Magnificent, who now ruled Syria, had taken it over as a mosque and forbidden any Christian to enter.

Other Holy Places were in the hands of different Christian sects, which at that time were even more numerous than they are today. Almost daily during her stay Angela would have passed the prison of Caiaphas which was then in the possession of the Armenians. Though owned by the Moslems, the church of the Holy Sepulchre itself was occupied by a multitude of Christian denominations. 'In the basilica,' wrote Felix Fabri, 'everyone, even the greatest heretic, can have his chapel if he pays a suitable tax to the Sultan.' The Moslems had no scruple in profiting from the devotion of the Christians, and it was in their interests to encourage as many different sects as they could find to establish themselves in some corner of the building. Sixteenth-century writers mention, among others, Syrians, Nubeans, Cafirs or Chaldaeans and Abyssinians. One traveller about this time observed that the Georgians wore great beards, and the Nestorians made the sign of the cross with one finger. The Syrians, he said, pronounced *y* as *u* and were consequently known as Surians. The Indians howled like wolves at the *Christe eleison*. Indeed, the smallest groups usually raised the greatest hubbub at prayer; and the most constant complaint of the pilgrims from the West was directed against the Abyssinians, for, as one writer says, 'from midnight until dawn they sang and played music, danced and raised a great deal of noise that never ceased'.

Payment had to be made to the Moslems for the

privilege of entering the church of the Holy Sepulchre, and the time pilgrims could pass within the building was rigidly controlled. Normally pilgrim parties entered in the evening. The Moslem keepers who guarded the building took their fee, unbarred the church, counted the party, and barred it again for the night, which, whether they liked it or not, the pilgrims were forced to spend inside the church.[1]

The distribution of the church among the different Christian bodies was much the same then as it is today, and there have been only incidental changes in the actual building. In shape it was an irregular quadrangle which was extended on the west side by a large semicircular bay that took in the traditional site of the sepulchre of Our Lord; and to the north a steep stone staircase led up to the place of the Crucifixion, which was shared by Orthodox and Catholics. Every incident in the Passion and Resurrection of Our Lord was commemorated by an altar. Angela prayed with fervour everywhere. This is the statement of Gian Battista Nazari, the Brescian notary, who in 1560 compiled the earliest life of St Angela from the depositions of her contemporaries. 'On reaching the place where Our Lord had been crucified,' he adds, 'she knelt down and covered with tears the ground that had been worthy to receive the precious

[1] At the time of the Saracen occupation of the Holy Places the custody of the church had been (and still is) in the hands of two distinguished Moslem families, called Nuseibeh and Judia. The former opened and closed the building, the latter guarded the key.

blood of Jesus Christ shed for sinners.' This statement of
Nazari's would have been obtained from Antonio
Romano, and in phrasing it echoes Ignatius Loyola's
account of his own visit.

The Franciscans had arranged a series of devotions
which with private prayer occupied the evening and the
entire night. At different altars, litanies, which were now
established as customary, were recited, and hymns sung
as the pilgrims proceeded round the church and took
their turn in more confined places to see and venerate
the rocks and stones which were associated with inci-
dents in the Passion. After the procession the pilgrims
made their confession, and then waited for the morning
Mass in the chapel of the Finding of the Holy Cross. If
any pilgrim was 'particularly tired' and unable to keep
the vigil, he was allowed 'to rest a little, either at the
Holy Sepulchre or at some other place'. The priests and
religious, including the Franciscan Tertiaries, passed the
vigil in the recitation of the Divine Office in the chapel
of the Apparition of Our Lord. At the morning Mass all
received Holy Communion.

The whole of the following morning was spent inside the church in sightseeing or in private devotion.
This also was the time allotted to unescorted visits to all
the sacred places within the building; to the chapel of
Adam below the site of Calvary; and at the entrance to
it, the tombs of Godfrey de Bouillon, the first Christian
King of Jerusalem, and his brother Baudouin, the leader
of the crusading armies. Behind, the cleft in the rock of
Calvary, dating from the earthquake that followed the

death of Our Lord, was pointed out to pilgrims. They were then shown the chapels dedicated to the mysteries of the Passion, the pink stone on which the Body of Our Lord was laid out for burial, and the place by the Sepulchre where, it was said, Our Lord appeared to Mary Magdalen on Easter morning. Behind the main part of the church, at the foot of a broad staircase, was the chapel of St Helena, who in the fourth century had discovered the True Cross and had identified the site of Calvary. 'It was only about midday,' says one writer, 'that the Turks returned, opened the church, made us all come out, counting each one and taking good care to leave nobody behind in the church.'[1]

It is important to remember that during the whole length of her stay in Palestine, Angela was almost totally blind. We are told by Agostino Gallo, as was noted earlier, that 'when she was led to places that aroused her most ardent devotion, she saw them with the eyes of her soul as if she had seen them with her bodily eyes'. These are exactly Angela's words, as Agostino testifies. She was never able to revisit Palestine, yet she never lost, but rather deepened, her love for the Holy Places, and on her return to Italy found means of evoking both the memories she had gathered and perhaps also the graces she had been granted during her pilgrimage. Throughout her life Angela showed an anxiety always to avoid any ostentation in her devotional practices. At Brescia she had prayed publicly in churches only as long as she could do so without attracting attention to herself, and then

[1] *The Pilgrimage of Christopher Radziwill to the Holy Land*, p. 72.

would return to her rooms in Antonio's house to continue her prayer unseen by others. This may explain why none of the many Franciscan writers on Jerusalem, with the single exception of Friar Giovanni di Calaona, recalls her visit. Moreover, in her desire to behave exactly like other pilgrims, she discontinued her rigorous abstinence and recovered sufficiently in health to make it possible for her eyesight also to recover. As she sat at table with other pilgrims, she would not have been singular in her diet; and except for the night passed in the church of the Holy Sepulchre, kept no vigils of prayer.[1]

Only at the end of the sixteenth century were the Stations, as they are now known, set in a regular pattern of devotion, and a clear distinction made between the last Stations inside the basilica and those outside it; nor was their number firmly established. It was then the custom to take the basilica itself as a starting-point for visits to other sacred places: to the Antonia, the Jerusalem residence of the Roman Governor, in the shadow of the great mosque of Omar, to Veronica's house, to the point at the turning of the road, marked by a chapel, where Our Lord had been assisted by the reluctant Simon the Cyrenean to drag the Cross along the last steep stretch of the road to Calvary. At the courtyard of the scourging there was then a church, and it was here that the medi-

---

[1] If Angela's recovery of sight was not miraculous, then she would seem to have suffered from a detachment of the retina in both eyes. This condition, often brought on by fatigue or undernourishment, causes complete blindness, and is known to right itself on improvement in general health.

eval pilgrim ended, and the modern pilgrim now begins, the *Via Crucis*. Some places were better authenticated than others, and outside the city the Moslems, with an eye to gain and some knowledge of Our Lord's life, had encouraged the more simple Christians to attach probable and improbable sites to places where it was known that Our Lord had worked miracles or passed the last days of His life. As a rule, pilgrims crossed the Kedron to the valley of Josaphat to visit Gethsemane and the underground church of Our Lady near by. Here, as they went down the dark staircase lit only by light from the entrance, they were shown on the left the tomb of St Joseph and on the right the tombs of St Anne and her husband St Joachim. In the choir of the church was the tomb of Our Lady, and, on the tombstone which formed an altar, the Franciscans, with the permission of the Armenian guardians, had the right to sing every Saturday of the year the Mass of the Feast of the Assumption. This was one of the religious functions the pilgrims unfailingly attended.

The visit to Bethlehem occupied only one day. A mile outside the town the pilgrims stopped at the tomb of Rachel, and from there looked across the valley to David's city on the right and to the church of the Shepherds on the left. The basilica itself, fortress-like in its exterior and unchanged since the time of Justinian, was entered through a low door which had been constructed for defence in the days of the Saracen invaders. Below the basilica was the cave, which had been used as a stable for the only inn in Bethlehem which served all travellers passing south to Hebron and Egypt. Now it was divided into three parts by pillars which supported the church above. In the centre was the manger and on the marble floor below the altar, framing a silver star, were the words that had the simplicity of a sentence from the Gospels or a clause from the Creed: *Hic de Virgine Maria Jesus Christus natus est.*

This was also the stable where David had kept his sheep and where Jerome had translated the Bible. Adjoining it was Jerome's tomb (his bones had been transferred to Rome) and the tombs of St Paula and St Eustochia.

The permission given to the pilgrims visiting the Holy Land expired after six weeks, but the Franciscans organized the itinerary so that most places could be seen at least once. In Jerusalem, on the first stage of their journey home, parties were led along the *Via Regis*— the old road used by the Patriarchs Elias, David, Isaias and Abraham himself—through Samaria into Galilee. This was also the road taken by St Joseph and Our Lady on the occasions when they came up from Galilee to celebrate the great Jewish festivals in Jerusalem. A short distance out, the caravan of pilgrims passed through Bethany and were shown the remains of Martha's house; and then at the end of the first day halted at Beroth where, according to tradition, Our Lady had discovered that her Child was missing from the party returning after the feast to Nazareth. As they entered Samaria the road passed through valleys with small crusading churches set among the vineyards and villages perched on the summits of the surrounding hills. On the second day a halt was usually made at Sichar, where Jacob's Well was guarded by Armenian priests; then the journey was resumed through Nablos and Sebastia— the church built in honour of John the Baptist was now a mosque—and across the plain of Ephraim and through the valley of Esdralon. Above Yanleh on a plateau was Nazareth. This was country not unlike the country south of Desenzano where Angela had lived the first forty years of her life; and the Lake of Galilee, which could be seen from the plateau, resembled in shape and in its surrounding hills and sudden changing moods her own Lake Garda.

Devotion to the Holy Child, which owed its current popularity to the preaching of the Franciscans, had given Renaissance artists one of their favourite subjects. The Madonna and Child was now replacing the Madonna alone in most of the churches of Italy. Angela, as will be seen, had a great interest in religious painting and knew many contemporary Italian artists. Moreover, she was a Franciscan Tertiary and had recently visited the shrine of Blessed Osanna, whose life and revelations gave a fresh stimulus to the devotion from Mantua to Brescia. Before she set out for the Holy Land she was prepared in spirit for her visit to Nazareth, one of the few places unspoilt by the Moslem occupation.

Elsewhere she had seen Christian churches transformed into mosques or into chapels for heretical sects. But at Nazareth the basilica was undamaged. Here in the crypt of the Grotto of the Annunciation and still in perfect condition were some of the finest mosaics in the world, representing scenes from both the Old and New Testaments, and also much of the history of the Church, particularly its Councils.

On their return the pilgrims were detained for eight days at Ramleh, a day's journey from Jaffa, for a report had reached Angela's party that pirates were lying in wait for their ship along the coast. Here the population was hostile and the accommodation for pilgrims comfortless. Eventually they sailed in fair weather, following the same course they had taken on their outward voyage. At Candia there was a long delay and here Angela recovered the sight of her eyes. That at least is the tradition, and it is certain that by the time she reached Venice her vision was normal. It was a sudden recovery in the sense that from seeing nothing she was able first to distinguish objects of light colour in her surroundings, and then by stages to discern faces and later colours, until at the end of her voyage her sight was completely restored.

At Candia the Viceroy of Crete boarded the pilgrim ship in order to travel to Venice and present his report on the government of the island to the Doge. Since Angela had set out on her pilgrimage the Saracen pirates had become more active, and to provide protection for the Viceroy, Angela's ship was joined by two armed Venetian merchantmen.

On 3 October, the eve of the feast of St Francis, only a few hours out from Candia, the convoy encountered a fierce storm lasting nine days. Angela's ship was separated from its escorts, both of which went down in the storm. The scene is one of the subjects of the artist of Desenzano, who shows Angela in her Franciscan habit standing motionless on the *castellum*, fearless as usual and in prayer, while the rest of the passengers and the entire ship's company are huddled below at the side of the mast in terror of the waves that threaten to swamp the ship. The helmsman was unable to keep his course, and though the ship weathered the storm he found himself cast onto the Barbary coast.

Angela's outward voyage had been without incident. Her return, even before her ship raised anchor, involved her in more dangers than the Franciscan handbooks on Palestine had prepared her to meet. Leaving the African coast almost at once for fear of pirates, the ship made for the Adriatic. For no stated reason, but probably through shortage of water after the long period at sea, the ship put in at the port of Durazzo, where the Turkish fleet lay at anchor. Two galleys put out to identify the strange ship and a message was sent by their commander to the Turkish captain, who demanded an interview with the Venetian Viceroy. Without waiting, the Viceroy raised anchor. Antonio Romano's account completes the story: 'God, who had decided through the intercession of Mother Angela's unceasing prayer to deliver us from danger, granted that immediately we left the port a following wind came up, so that we made a town on the Slovenian coast and soon afterwards reached Venice itself, where we stayed for some time.'

7

Venice and Rome

On her return from Jerusalem Angela stayed in Venice several weeks. For the first few days she lodged with the religious of the Holy Sepulchre. Adjoining the church was a hospital, where the sick pilgrims, unable immediately to continue their journey, were nursed by the Sisters. But Angela had little peace here. The miraculous escape of the pilgrims' ship with the Viceroy on board was attributed to her prayers. Tales of her personal holiness were passed round the city, and she was visited by priests and religious leaders, anxious to meet her and hear her conversation. The excitement caused by her presence left her with no privacy, and after a few days she moved to the Hospital of Incurables. But again the visits were resumed. 'Monks, laymen, women, priests and pious folk came to her incessantly; and also leading citizens, anxious to discover more about her life.' Always her appeal was to every class of people, for she was gifted with sympathetic understanding of the lives of others. It was this that attracted the citizens to her, both 'princes and the common crowd,' as one biographer writes. Never in her life did she claim any special enlightenment for the guidance of others, and there is no authenticated deposition that ascribes to her the gift of prophecy or prevision. She was a child of the country with a shrewdness refined by prayer and constant penance. Her insight into character had developed from her own dealings with others, and had come early in life when as a young girl she had been left an orphan in the care of her uncle.

The reason for Angela's stay in Venice is not given by Antonio Romano. It has been suggested that Antonio had business there. Possibly also Angela, while nursing the sick, had hoped to find in Venice time for prayer in obscurity that she was less likely to have in Brescia. There can be no doubt that in the Holy Land she had asked God for a definition of the message given to her at Brudazzo. She was now in her fiftieth year and her next decision, namely, to visit Rome, was made not merely with the purpose of completing, so to speak, her visit to Jerusalem but also with the intention of obtaining the Pope's approval for the establishment of a Company of virgins such as she had seen in her vision. Now, owing to her connections and her personal power of attraction, this principal aim of her life had become possible to achieve.

Once again, her career ran parallel with that of Ignatius Loyola, who would have been known to many of her more important callers in Venice, and whose mission at this period sent him to the same cities as Angela, set on the same intention of finding the exact purpose which God had for him and his companions.

Ignatius was determined that his own Company should not bear his name, and it is certain that Angela, who was as long a time in forming hers, had come to the same determination. Already she was looking for a heavenly patroness who would give her name to the

Company she was about to form. Some writers have improved, so to speak, on the vision of Brudazzo and have placed St Ursula at the head of the band of angels that she saw there. But there is no solid ground for this. It is more probable that during her stay in Venice she frequently heard discussed the legend of St Ursula and her fellow martyrs. This northern saint had been adopted with enthusiasm by the people of Italy, and especially by Venice. Behind the church of SS. John and Paul, close to where Angela lived, was the school of St Ursula, founded in the fifteenth century for craftsmen and artists. Here, Vittore Carpaccio, taking the facts of the story from the *Legenda Sanctorum*, had decorated the walls of the building with a series of nine canvases that told the complete story of Ursula. The work was begun in 1488—there is a record of a payment made to him on 18 November that year—and was completed in 1495. Careless of chronology, Carpaccio had first painted the arrival of St Ursula at Cologne and then followed this vast canvas with her glorification after death. The last in the series was Ursula's dream and her interview with the English prince: and between the first and the last came the audience of the English envoys with King Maurus; their return to England, and, most significantly for Angela, the meeting of Ursula and her virgins with the Pope at the gates of Rome.

Although not a Venetian himself, Carpaccio was perhaps the most honoured man in the city. In another series on St George in the school named after this saint, he had set this hero-patron of the Crusaders against the

background of Venice. In both works his characters
were citizens of the time—Capraccio could not resist
portraying St Jerome as a rich Venetian scholar sitting
in his comfortable study without a hint of asceticism—
the drapery, architecture, ornaments, interiors, even the
colour and grain of the marbles, are taken from the
Venice of his day. More than any other painter, he re-
created the atmosphere and perspectives of the city.
Now he was at the height of his fame, but an old and
sick man; in fact he died within a year of Angela's
return to Brescia. Whether the two met is not known,
but Angela would have heard praised by her friends his
work in the school of St Ursula, and now with her
recovered sight would have been able to study in detail
the pictures that told the story she had learned as a child
from her father. These paintings helped her to interpret
the legend of St Ursula in the context and background
of her day, and probably determined the name she was
to give her Company.

While at Venice, Angela was asked by members of the
Doge's Council to remain in the city and take charge
of the Hospital of Incurables where she was staying. A
few years before Angela's return from Palestine it had
been refounded by John Cajetan, a saintly priest six
years younger than Angela and a native of Vicenza.
Cajetan had been ordained in the year Angela had left
Desenzano to live in Brescia and had gathered about him
a number of priests who lived together by rule and
sought out the aged poor and sick, establishing for them
modern hospitals, first in Verona and later in other

cities of northern Italy. After taking over the old hospital in Venice he had extended it, but had left the city for Rome twelve months before Angela's return from Palestine. Angela's reputation for the care of the sick in Brescia must have followed her to Venice, for it is unlikely that she would have been offered charge of the largest, best-known and most modern hospital in the city before she was scarcely known to the Council. Angela, however, had no hesitation in refusing. She was clear in her mind that no matter how much Venice needed her, Brescia was her home and had first claim on her. A successor to John Cajetan was found in another saintly priest, a Venetian, Jerome Aemiliani, just a year older than Cajetan. It is not unlikely that Angela's advice was sought in this appointment. Certainly Jerome would have been among her callers, for he was frequently at the hospital. Through the worst years of famine and plague he had nursed the sick of Venice and had then taken charge of the orphan children of the poor. Hand in hand with this work went the instruction of children in Christian doctrine and it is claimed that he was the first priest to draw up a Catechism in the form of question and answer.

The conversations Angela had with Jerome are likely to have confirmed her in her vocation, and to have helped her to develop her own methods of teaching. We know that Jerome, possibly at Angela's instigation, later established a house of his Congregation at Brescia. There they would have met frequently.

Among Angela's other callers at Venice was the Patriarch, and as pressure on her to stay increased, she feared that he might be persuaded to order her to take over the management of the Hospital of Incurables. As a Franciscan Tertiary under obedience to her director, Angela would have found it difficult to ignore such a command, so with Antonio she left Venice, passing through Padua and Vicenza probably on her first and second day. The exact date of Angela's departure from Venice is not known, but it was probably shortly after the middle of November, for she arrived back at Brescia on the 25th of that month.

There had never been any doubt in Angela's mind that her vocation lay in Brescia. In successive years she was to reject invitations from Prince Luigi Gonzaga, from the Council of Venice and from the Pope himself, to work respectively in Castiglione, Venice and Rome. In all these three cities she was offered the support of the ruling sovereign, yet she declined their invitations unhesitatingly. She was now firmly resolved to found her Company, and to found it in Brescia. Time was pressing on her and she had become very aware of this during her visit to the East.

In December 1522 the island of Rhodes had fallen after an heroic defence by the Knights Templar, who had repulsed the Turks twenty-three times before yielding for lack of ammunition. This Turkish conquest had exposed the Adriatic and Italy to the heathen, and Pope Adrian VI, knowing full well what it meant for Europe, broke down on receiving the news, crying out, 'Alas, for Christendom.' In the following year, as Angela set out on her pilgrimage to Blessed Osanna's shrine in Mantua, Sweden had yielded to the Lutherans. At Durazzo, on her return from Palestine, she had encountered the Turkish fleet that was threatening the West. In Rome itself spies had recently been arrested, and unfounded rumours were constantly heard that their armies had landed at this or that place in Apulia. Belgrade was already taken. Hungary, cut off from supplies by sea, was threatened. The Pope in vain appealed to the ruling princes to end their quarrels and unite in a crusade. But it was Angela's own country, particularly the Duchy of Milan, coveted relentlessly by Francis I of France and the Emperor Charles V, that made peace impossible. Meanwhile, with every fresh victory won against a divided Europe, the Turks were said to call out, 'And now to Rome!'

Adrian VI, a Dutchman and the last non-Italian Pope, had died of grief on 14 September 1523. Instead of uniting Europe against the Turks he had seen Francis I prepare for an invasion of Italy, and had received from him barely-veiled threats to set up an anti-Pope if the Pope did not support his ambitions. Reluctantly, in the August before he died, on the feast of Our Lady of the Snow, Adrian had ridden out early in the morning, protected by his Swiss Guard against threatened French attempts to assassinate him, to S. Maria Maggiore, where he proclaimed a Holy League, consisting of Venice, Austria, the Emperor and the Duke of Milan, not against the Turks but against France. On the very day he died the French crossed into Italy. The inscription below his tomb in S. Maria dell'Anima, the church of the German nation, summarizes the pathos of his life: 'Alas, how much do the efforts of the best men depend upon time and opportunity.'[1]

Until the problem of Milan was settled, there was no chance of peace or a new crusade. Angela, foreseeing that her adopted city of Brescia was going to be the centre of war, had become anxious to return. But for the moment Brescia was unmolested. Taking advantage of the respite, she visited Rome. A Holy Year had been proclaimed by Adrian's successor, Clement VII. In the Bull, opening with the phrases, *Inter sollicitudines et curas nobis incumbentes,*[2] and dated 23 December 1524, just four weeks after Angela had reached Brescia, the Pope expressed his hope that by stirring up religious enthusiasm he would be preparing the ground for reform in the Church. War, the plague in Rome, the threat of Turkish landings, might have deterred him from the announcement of a Jubilee, but he persevered. 'With all these cares in mind', the Pope lightened the conditions for obtaining the Jubilee indulgence. Confession, Holy Communion, visits to the Roman Basilicas and the prescribed prayers had to be said, but almsgiving, though encouraged, was no longer required. Through custom, however, most pilgrims gave offerings to the poor on their way to Rome or in the city itself. Few indeed have expressed better than Angela herself the spiritual benefits

[1] *Proh Dolor, quantum refert in quae tempora vel optimi cuiusque virtus incidat.*

[2] Printed in Rome, 1524. British Museum, 5016 aaa. 59 (2).

of this practice. 'God is our goal,' she was to tell her companions, possibly with the recollection of the Holy Year still fresh in her memory, 'and we advance to it by almsgiving. By this means we often withdraw a man from vice. If he is already good, we encourage him to become better.' And then with remarkable shrewdness she adds: 'Almsgiving is a kind of trading in souls, by which charity draws them to virtue and then ties them to it by an unbreakable bond.'

Angela set out from Brescia in company with a group of other pilgrims that included Antonio Romano and two priests. 'Desiring to see the holy relics,' writes Antonio, 'she undertook the journey.' This is the first direct reference we have to Angela's great attachment to relics, particularly to the relics of the early Christian martyrs, that took such a large place in her devotional life. In this she was a spiritual child of her age, and shared with it a simple belief in the healing power of relics. In Venice she heard of the offer of two thousand ducats made by the Republic for the recovery of Our Lord's tunic that had been stolen from the city. On her way to Rome the story would have been told of the war between Perugia and Siena for the alleged wedding-ring of Our Lady. Recently Rome had increased its treasury of relics. Amid wild rejoicings Pius II had brought there the head of St Andrew, and later Innocent VIII had acquired the Holy Lance.

There were two principal routes used by the pilgrims to Rome from north Italy. The route by Lucca and Siena was the easier and more popular, but it is less

likely to have been taken by Angela, for it lay too far
to the west of Brescia. The second route passed through
Rimini. There it divided. The old road crossed the
Apennines through Urbino, Assisi, and Foligno: an
alternative route branched down the coast to Fano and
Loreto and then rejoined the old road at Foligno. From
there it was a short and easy journey to Rome.

It can be assumed that Angela, either on her way to
Rome or on her return, visited Loreto, for it had long
been established as the second shrine of Christendom.
Here was the Holy House, once occupied by Our Lady
and St Joseph at Nazareth, and now resting on a hill
overlooking the Adriatic a few miles inland from
Ancona. It was a place of continuous prayer and in
recent years the exterior of the house, now enclosed
in a basilica, had been decorated by marbles, sculptured
in relief by some of the most famous artists of the
Renaissance.[1]

Already by the eleventh century these routes to Rome
were well supplied with hospices. Few survive today,
but at San Geneso, on the route from Loreto to Rome,
there is an early hostel recently restored and now used
as a mill. This, like many, had been endowed; in other
places, where there were no hostels, pious bequests had
eased the burdens of the journey. At Piacenza, for instance, and at Lucca, the Countess Mathilda of Tuscany

---

[1] According to legend, the house, consisting of two rooms,
with a barrel roof, was transported from Nazareth by angels.
Another tradition maintains that it was brought over by the
crusaders in the twelfth century and reconstructed at Loreto.

in the eleventh century had made provision for all Scandinavian pilgrims passing through these towns to be given as much free wine as they were able to consume.

On their arrival in Rome, pilgrims made first for the ancient Basilica of St Peter, with its fine portico decorated with mosaics, now just twelve hundred years old and to be demolished shortly after Angela's death by Nicholas V. In the district surrounding it most of the hostels were to be found, and there special stores of food were laid in for the pilgrims. In a successful year of Jubilee as many as 400,000 people made their way to Rome—more than eight times the normal population of the city. Here also cardinals, prelates and court officials lived. It was a dense area and its poor dwellings contrasted with the magnificent houses of the nobility, decorated on the street-front with stucco paintings, in the Via Giulia across the Tiber. The Aventine was still without private dwellings; only a few rich citizens had their homes on the Quirinal, Esquiline and Caelian hills. The Palatine and Capitoline, with their immense ruins of ancient Rome, were still wild and unkempt and served as quarries for the new builders.

There is little in the paintings and records of the time concerning the Jubilee of 1525, but a fine engraving exists of the opening procession of the Holy Year just fifty years later. The ceremonial is unchanged. It shows the Pope being carried to St Peter's for the ceremony in which he knocks three times on the Basilica door with a silver hammer. The square is crowded with pilgrims, and the dome of the new Basilica, half completed, is seen behind the façade of the ancient church.

It is not known whether Angela was in Rome for the opening of the Holy Year. It is merely recorded that she went there for the Jubilee. To gain the indulgence she had to visit the seven main churches. In the Basilica of St John Lateran, *Sacrosancta Lateranensis Ecclesia*, was preserved what was then regarded as the finest collection of relics in the world, which included the heads of St Peter and St Paul, the largest fragment of the wood of the True Cross, brought to Rome by St Helena, a piece of the couch on which Our Lord reclined at the Last Supper, a thorn from the crown of thorns, a fragment from Longinus' lance, and other relics of the Passion. Only modern writers have cast doubts on the authenticity of these relics, many of which today have been withdrawn from veneration. But at the time of Angela as well as today, relics, authenticated or not, were, so to speak, the starting-points for prayer and meditation and brought closer to the devout imagination the details of Our Lord's life and the life of His mother and the saints. Still within the precincts of the Lateran Basilica was the Scala Santa, the steps up which Our Lord mounted for his interview with Pilate. Pilgrims then, as now, ascended these steps on their knees, and in this and in many other ways Angela was given the opportunity, as it were, to make complete what she had missed in her visit to Palestine.

While at Rome Angela met a priest who in the previous year had been on the same pilgrimage with her to the Holy Land. This happened accidentally during her visit to one of the Basilicas. His name is given as Mgr della Puglia, and he was one of Clement VII's chamberlains. By his means an audience was arranged with the Pope, who, in spite of the unceasing anxieties of his reign, took pleasure, and perhaps recreation, in seeing all who sought his presence. Clement VII, Giulio de' Medici, unlike most of his family, was good-looking. As a cardinal he had gained a reputation for courtesy to all classes of persons. Tall, graceful and in good health, he was only forty-eight at the time he met Angela. In his piety he had forbidden professional jesters to perform at the banquet following his coronation; nevertheless, he was a patron of the arts and music. Certainly he was not a Pope for the times. Prosaic and vacillating, he kept his own uncertain counsels. 'The most secretive man in the world,' said one of his courtiers. 'I have never spoken to anybody whose sayings were harder to decipher.'[1] His parsimonious character did not endear him to the Romans; but on the other hand he was generous in his almsgiving, particularly during the plague, which was at its height during the Holy Year.

Indeed, owing to the plague and the unsettled condition of Italy, the Jubilee of 1525 was not the success Clement VII had expected. Yet it brought to Rome two founders of new religious Orders who were to receive from the Pope the blessing and official encouragement that they needed for a work which was to add considerable strength to the later efforts to combat heresy in

[1] Heine, Briefe, 86, 401; Pastor, IX, 249.

the old world. About the same time that Angela was received in private audience, the Franciscan hermit, Matteo da Bascio, a lay brother, came down from the mountains of Umbria to ask the Pope's permission to follow the primitive rule of St Francis which, in his view, had been betrayed by the Observantine Brethren. At the time he had only his own case in mind; there was no question of gathering followers or founding an Order. When Clement VII gave him the authorization he sought he was unaware that he was promoting the foundation of a religious Order, later to be known as the Capuchins. For in the next year two Observantine Brethren, one of them a priest, attached themselves to Brother Matteo; others followed, attracted by their example of a hard life and by their striking appearance, with hoods, bare feet, and crucifixes fastened in the girdles that held up their sackcloth habits.

At her own audience with Clement VII Angela appears to have spoken of her plans of founding a Company of women for the work of Christian instruction of the young and for the charitable assistance of the sick. As with Brother Matteo, the Pope approved in principle, but there was still no question of a formal *Rule*. All that Angela sought for the moment was the Pope's blessing on a scheme, still incomplete in her own conception. As in her earlier meetings with persons of high rank, Angela impressed the Pope with her combination of worldly wisdom and remarkable saintliness. It is recorded that after her audience the Pope turned to Mgr della Puglia with the words, 'Is this how you tell the Pope about the visitors you introduce?' 'Perhaps,' the chamberlain replied, trying to excuse himself, 'my own admiration for Sister Angela made me speak too well of her.' 'Not well enough, not well enough,' retorted Clement, and he began praising her as a person of the most rare gifts. He revealed that he had asked her to stay in Rome in order to take charge of charitable works in the city, and that Angela had pleaded with him that her mission lay in Brescia, and begged Clement's leave to return there.[1]

No further details are recorded of this visit. On her return to Brescia, Angela resumed her work in the city. Her life now moved more rapidly towards the foundation of her Company, but there were further interruptions due to war. Moreover, greater clarification was needed in prayer before she was able to realize the vision granted to her at Brudazzo.

[1] Carlo Doneda, *Vita della B. Angela Merici*, p.36.

8

Francesco Sforza

Writers on St Angela find it difficult to explain why on
her return from Rome she did not immediately set about
the foundation of her Company. In Venice she had all
the appearance of being impatient to set about the work;
in Rome she had received the Pope's approval for the
project as she put it before him; yet it was another nine
years before the Company took shape. During this time
she went on two pilgrimages; at home she continued
her works of charity. It is a problem that so bewildered
some later biographers that they have introduced into
her story a vision in which Our Lord is alleged to have
appeared to the saint some time during this period and
scolded her for her remissness in carrying out his commission. But there is little substance in this story, which
is probably an interpolation of a statement of her friend
Gabriel Cozzano that Angela was 'urged and commanded to found her Order'.[1] The causes for the delay
lie more in the difficulty she experienced in finding the
right companions and, to a large extent also, in the
troubled state of Brescia.

Although from the first days after her return to
Desenzano from Salo Angela had gathered helpers about
her, she had made no attempt to force on them her own

[1] cf. Gabriel Cozzano, *Epistola Confortatoria* in the Mother
Cecilia Lubienska, *Ojczyna sw Angeli* (1935), p. 353.

way of life, nor had she tried to hold them together. Whoever came forward, worked with her. Probably group succeeded group in Brescia as happened in Desenzano and on several occasions she appears to have had about her a nucleus of women that might have formed a Company. There is little known about most of them, but it is probable that she experienced the same kind of successive failures as did Ignatius Loyola, who only on his third or fourth attempt gathered and held together a suitable band of like-minded companions. The little we know of Angela's associates suggests this was her experience also. In her *Rule* she insists, probably with the memory of her own early disappointments in mind, that very detailed inquiry is to be made into the character of those seeking admission. 'Every effort', she writes, 'is to be made to get the minutest information concerning their life and habits.' Indeed, none of the names of her earliest friends in Brescia is among the first members of the Company. Moreover, as with Ignatius Loyola, her ideas developed slowly. It took both saints many years to advance from the first steps they made to work with men or women of the same ideals to the formation of a new religious Order;[1] both were feeling their way towards a revolutionary pattern of unenclosed religious life. To interpret their slow progress as a failure to correspond with grace is a misreading of

[1] St Ignatius hung up his sword and dagger before the statue of Our Lady at Monserrat on 24 March 1522; formal approval of his Order was given in a Bull of Paul III dated 27 September 1540, more than eighteen years later.

history. The divine rebuke which Angela is said to have received is a piece of unauthentic interpolation. No more rapid progress could be expected if the foundations of the Company were to be solidly laid.

Moreover, Angela returned to a bitterly divided and suffering Brescia. Pilgrims on their way to Rome in the year of Jubilee had seen nothing but disaster and destruction in the north of Italy.

Once again the Duchy of Milan had become the centre of war. In May 1524, when Angela had set out for the Holy Land, the French had been driven out of Italy. When she was in Jerusalem the Emperor Charles V had pursued them into France, but before the walls of Marseilles he had suffered a reverse. Francis I rallied his armies, and before Angela was back in Brescia he had marched on Milan and had occupied the city. As Angela left for Rome Francis was besieging Pavia. Clement VII, always unfortunate in his alliances, had sided with the French king, taking for granted his complete conquest of Italy. Then suddenly fortunes were reversed and on 25 February, possibly while Angela was making her visit to the Roman churches, Francis was utterly defeated by the Emperor, who now ominously threatened Clement VII that he would side with Luther and the heretics if the Pope did not yield to all his political demands.

On her return from Rome Angela found Brescia and other northern cities overrun with disbanded and disorganized mercenaries—Swiss, German and Scottish—making their livelihood by plunder. They became the dread of all the cities through which they fought on their way back to the frontier. Francis' own personal bodyguard of Scottish archers, left to their own devices, eventually passed through Milan up the Val Cannobia, where they were trapped by snow in the Simplon Pass. There they settled in the village of Gurra, where their descendants today are still distinguished by their Celtic features and the Italianized form of Scottish names.[1]

From Antonio Romano's house Angela continued her work. The many urgent calls on her time and strength further explain her delay in founding her Company. Many families had left the city during the disturbances of war. Also Brescia, situated at the end of the Alpine pass into Germany through the Trento valley, received its share of passing mercenary bands. At the same time the poor of the city were calling for bread outside the Podesta's house; moreover, there were many plague victims. The Hospital of Incurables was already filled and the Ospitale Grande, only five minutes from her house, near St Agatha's, was caring for more than three hundred and fifty patients. Many of Angela's friends gave their help, wearing masks against infection, and taking turns to sit at night at the bedside of the sick.

At home we have her host's own testimony of her life at this time. 'While she stayed at my house,' Antonio Romano writes, 'and this was for about fourteen

[1] *Sunday Times*, 7 August 1960, p. 5: 'The Lost Clan', by John Cathorp. About eight hundred dialect words of the people of Gurra are Gaelic in origin.

years, she used to sleep on a mat, using a piece of wood under her head for a pillow. I do not recollect ever having seen her eat meat, but only fruit and vegetables, or drink anything but water.'

Milan in these years was also afflicted by the plague. In the last nine months of 1524 it had taken toll of 80,000 inhabitants. Francesco Sforza, the ruling Duke, fared no better from the Emperor than he had done from Francis I. Within a year of the battle of Pavia his position had become intolerable. In the height of his troubles he sought Angela's advice and comfort.

Although he had succeeded as a small boy to the duchy in 1514, Francesco had not taken possession of it until 4 April 1521, when he entered Milan amid wild rejoicings and the firing of guns. Citizens had showered jewels on him to pay for his mercenary army, but within two years his misfortunes began. Riding on the road to Monza, an attempt had been made to assassinate him. The following year, when Francis I's forces swept into Italy, he had withdrawn to Cremona rather than offer useless resistance with a disheartened army and a plague-stricken people. Charles V had eventually restored him, but only as his vassal, subject to the payment of 500,000 ducats a year. Then Charles had suspected him of treason and had besieged him in his castle at Milan where, after five months, he surrendered for lack of provisions.

Deprived of his duchy, without resources of men or money, and without a friend on whom he could rely, Francesco passed through Brescia on his way to

Cremona. During the nineteen days of his stay there he resided in the convent next to the church of St Barnabas. Although a young man, he suffered ill health which he ascribed to the poisoned dagger of his would-be assassin. Already in Milan he had heard of the great work done by Angela and now he asked to meet her. Angela visited him. It is not known how often they met on this occasion, but they came to know each other well enough for easy intimacy to be established. Francesco told her at length about his manifold troubles and asked Angela to accept him as her spiritual child; and going further, he begged her to take his duchy 'under her protection'. Angela promised her prayers and henceforth she and the Duke took every opportunity of meeting.

This was the lowest ebb of the Duke's fortunes. Among the subjects they discussed would certainly have been the condition of Rome, for in the June before they met the Spanish forces, unable to squeeze any more booty out of the Duchy of Milan, had marched south, more like a rabble than an army, and passing through Florence had entered Rome. Clement VII fled and there followed the worst sacking of the city since the invasion of the Goths. Possibly taking this as her theme, Angela, as her biographers say, spoke to the Duke about the futility of human glory, just at this moment when the magnificence of Renaissance Rome was in danger of being lost for ever.

Was it merely for spiritual guidance that Francesco was so anxious to meet Angela? Her biographers say that it was Angela's reputation, not primarily for wise counsel but principally as a peacemaker, that attracted the Duke to her. The latest disasters he had suffered arose from suspicions in the mind of Charles V that Francesco had allied himself to Clement VII, and this had been his excuse for sacking Milan once again and besieging Francesco in his castle. There is no letter yet discovered to prove any intervention on the part of Angela in the quarrel, but the intense admiration that Francesco formed for Angela and the reliance he henceforth placed on her may well be explained by Angela's part in healing the breach between the Duke and the Emperor. She was the greatest of all the peacemakers of her time and is never known to have failed when she attempted to reconcile warring individuals. But the fact remains that within a very short time of Francesco's stay in Brescia, Charles had restored him to his duchy. When Angela passed through Milan in the following year, Francesco pressed her to stay in the castle he had recently recovered. Perhaps it is not too far-fetched to see in this invitation the desire of the Duke to make a public gesture of his indebtedness to Angela for the restoration of his rights and domains.

Part of the secret of Angela's power of sympathy lay in her very simplicity. She attributed nothing to herself. 'To do so', she wrote (these were her last words of advice to her daughters), 'is to ask God to abandon us. In order to become an instrument in his hands we must be of no account in our own eyes.' The statement, like every other expression of a fundamental principle in the spiritual life, is ordinary, but the application of it to her own conduct remains in large measure the secret of her influence over others.

In dealing with all classes Angela had in mind the particular state of the individuals who sought her advice. With a natural sympathy for the poor as well as for princes—this was a quality of her sanctity that made so great an impression on the Venetians—she remembered in all her dealings with the great that she did not belong to their society by birth. She was neither a snob, nor what, in modern jargon, is called an inverted snob. When later she founded her Company, she admitted to it both noble ladies and their servants and would allow no difference in their observance of the *Rule*. It had been her experience that God made no distinction of class in his distribution of special graces and that none had a prerogative of virtue. On a human level this was all part of her basic shrewdness.

Agostino Gallo was a witness to her activity at this time. 'Throughout her life', he writes, 'she was always helping people. They used to come and consult her about changing their lives, or to seek her comfort in their distress: also they asked her advice in making their wills, in taking wives or marrying their sons and daughters. And besides, there was never any lack of people who needed her to make peace, between wife and husband, father and son, brother and brother. She would advise and console them all as much as she could, so that her work seemed more divine than human.'

Not infrequently, from her first days in Brescia and more especially after her return from Palestine and

Rome, she was sought out for counsel in cases of alleged mystics and clairvoyants. It was an age of false as well as of true mystics, and it is interesting to compare her approach with that of Ignatius Loyola. Much the same fundamental principles appear both in Angela's *Rule* and in the *Exercises*. While both treasured and experienced special graces in prayer, and both knew and revered remarkable mystics, yet both insisted also that, without a firm purpose of never offending God, growth in Christ was impossible. 'What a mistake some of the faithful make,' she is reported to have said, 'when people give all their attention to saying long prayers, running hither and thither to hear long sermons, to assist at the ceremonies of the Church, attend Sodality meetings, and yet at the same time neglect to conform to the simple prescriptions of the divine law touching their state of life.' And she concludes: 'The first maxim we must put in practice is, above all things, to avoid offending God so that he will grant us the grace of loving Him as he deserves.'

All this time Angela was forging the instrument of her apostolate. With Ignatius Loyola many years elapsed between the first application of the principles learned at Manresa and their final formulation in the *Exercises*. In the interval he had gathered experience in his work of instructing both men and women in the Christian life, drawing them from a life of frivolity or sin; and after that, if his disciples were capable of it, to a more personal following of Our Lord, and finally to the highest ideal of self-sacrifice. This would appear

to have been very little different from the method of
Angela. Her inspiration was not given the same sharp
formulation, but throughout her *Rule*, and in the other
documents she left her Company, the same framework
protrudes. This is only to be expected, since their
apostolate lay in the same milieu and was undertaken
with the same aims and encountered the same difficulties. Striking conversions followed Angela's unceasing activity and indifferent Christians were induced to
receive the sacraments. Angela, however, unlike Ignatius, did not write down or dictate to any followers the
secret of her influence. But in other ways the similarity
between the two saints is very close, and their spirit is
the same. The opening phrase of Ignatius's *Constitutions*,
'Those who serve God in this Company', reflects the
purpose laid down by Angela for admission into her
own Order: 'To enter this Company it is necessary to
have a firm intention of serving God.'

However, Angela's foundation lay ahead. In the year
1529 she made her first pilgrimage to Varallo in the Val
Sesia. The unsettled condition of Milan and the mercenary bands still lying about the approaches to the
Alps had made the pilgrimage impossible before this
year. And in any case Angela was delayed in Brescia by
the devastation caused by the Duke of Brunswick's
forces, who in the spring of 1528 had come down
through Trento along Lake Garda, sacking all the towns
she had known in her childhood and her first missionary
years, Salo, Lonato and Gavardo. 'Five thousand ducats
or fire and sword,' he had called out before the gates

of Salo. In June these Germans had passed through Brescia 'with such tremor that it seemed as though the world had come tumbling down, and every living soul had to pay a tax for the support of the exhibition'.

When finally Angela was able to leave for Varallo she sought there the completion of the graces given to her in the Holy Land. At the same time, she was answering an invitation of Francesco Sforza to continue the personal work she had done for him in Brescia.

9

Varallo

The pilgrimage Angela made in 1529 to Varallo, the New Jerusalem as it was called, was the first of two visits to the shrine. Here she appears finally to have overcome the difficulties and hesitations that still lay in her path, for after the second visit she set about the foundation of her Company. From now until her death there is no record of other pilgrimages she may have made. At Varallo she reached the goal of her lifelong search for the clarification of the message she received at Brudazzo.

The two pilgrimages to Varallo are as important in her life as her visit to the Holy Land. Indeed, she received here the guidance of the kind she had so long and so constantly given to others and had waited until now, the last decade of her life, to be given herself.

The road to Varallo from Brescia lay west through Milan and Novara; there it turned north through the broad plain until it entered the valley of the Sesia, then continued past Briona, Fara, Ghemme and Romagno. Here it began to climb, following the river through a narrow pass covered with limes and chestnuts. It was a valley of short, stocky, isolated, sub-Alpine people with as much German as Italian blood, independent and more ready to accept heresy with its foreign associations than the Lombards of the plain.

At the head of the valley, where the Sesia was joined by the river Mastallone, lay Varallo encircled by mountains of the Monte Rosa range. Immediately to the north the small town with its narrow streets and frescoed walls was overhung by a conical hill, some five hundred feet high, which in 1491 was visited by a remarkable and aged Observantine Friar, Bernardino Caimi.

Formerly the Guardian of the Holy Places in Palestine, Bernardino Caimi had travelled through all the northern hills of Lombardy in search of a site for the building of a new Jerusalem. The reasons for his choice of Varallo are obscure. Some writers say that its similarity of the hill site to Jerusalem determined him, and others have seen in Monte Sacro, the new name given to the hill, an exact counterpart of the Holy City, with the Sesia taking the place of the Kedron and Lake Orta the Sea of Galilee, and even the Fathers of St Bernard Mentone in the Graian and Pennine Alps standing for the ancient Levites. The parallel is too far-fetched to be convincing. Still others have explained the choice by means of a vision in which Bernardino is alleged to have seen the old Jerusalem on the hill then known as La Parete, and was confirmed in his choice by the discovery of a stone, still seen in the Varallo chapel of the Holy Sepulchre, resembling exactly in shape and dimensions the stone covering the burial place of Our Lord in Jerusalem.

Although these stories may have helped Angela in her devotion—and it must be remembered that owing to her temporary blindness she had been unable to see the real Jerusalem—she would also have appreciated the more obvious reason for the foundation. At the end of many passes into northern Italy from Switzerland and Germany, shrines had been set up as spiritual bulwarks against the inroads of heresy. In some of these valleys old medieval heresies lingered on. Here also, because of the closeness of the people both in character and in sympathy to the Germans, was the best seeding ground of the new doctrines. With shrewd foresight saintly men of the century were building shrines in these valleys to fortify the faith of the people, at Varese, Locarno, Orta, Oropa, Graglia, S. Ignazio and S. Giovanni di Andorno—making them, as it were, strongpoints on the frontiers of the Church; and it is likely that Bernardino Caimi had in mind the protection of Novara and Milan when he selected for his new Jerusalem the head of this valley of half-German people. It was with the same instinct, also, that a few years after Angela's death the greatest Council of the Church was summoned to meet at Trento, a few days' journey from Torbole at the head of Lake Garda. Already some approaches to Italy, the Val Bregnalia and the Valle di Poschiavo, for instance, had been lost, while others, won by the heretics in the first attack, were recovered at the Counter-Reformation.

Since Angela had first settled there, Brescia, at the military cross-roads of northern Italy, had been threatened for many years by the northern heretics and it was vital that Angela's city should be held for the Church. There is a certain suggestion of importunity in the way her second visit to Varallo followed fast on her first, as though she saw the Company she was about to found as a weapon against heresy in the hands of the Church. She had seen heterodox preachers in the cities of northern Italy—Lutherans left in the wake of invading armies—while old heretics, like the Waldenses, gained greater freedom because the occupying forces contained officers of their faith. With the constant changes in their overlords, civic authorities were adopting a more tolerant attitude towards them. Angela's warning against false teachers in her *Counsels* can only be a repetition of her constant advice throughout the last period of her life: 'You will have to defend your flock against counterfeit religions and heretics. When you hear that any preacher or other person has the name of being tainted with heresy and preaches any doctrines not commonly received in the Church, you must prevent your daughters from going to hear them.'[1] In this denunciation she was not before her time. Calvin had already preached at Ferrara and, under patronage of the Duchess, had already made many proselytes, and it was only a year after Angela's death, and perhaps owing to her insistent warning against heresy, that an inquiry was eventually made into the activities of Lutheran and Zwinglian preachers who were busy propagating new doctrines in Brescia, Milan and Pavia. Among their converts were Augustinian and Franciscan friars who acted as agents for the dissemination of the works of the reformers that had already been translated into Italian. 'Consider', Angela warns her followers, 'that the devil does not sleep, but seeks our ruin in a thousand ways.' Then, as though placing herself

[1] Seventh Counsel

and her newly formed order at the foot of the crucifix, as no doubt she did in spirit and in anticipation at Varallo, she concludes: 'In these dangerous and pestilential times you will find no other refuge than at the feet of Jesus Christ.'[1]

At Varallo during her first visit, the chapel of the Crucifixion, one of the finest of the forty-five chapels and shrines that eventually comprised the New Jerusalem, was nearing completion; and here Angela must have prayed frequently on both her pilgrimages. This was perhaps the finest of the works executed at Varallo by Gaudenzio Ferrari, the artist from Valduzza in the Sesia Valley, who had been engaged to direct the building of the shrine. Frescoes with more than one hundred and fifty figures cover the walls of the chapel and there are another twenty-six life-size figures in terra cotta, two of them on horseback in the foreground. The knights, soldiers and horsemen are in the costumes of the day, with their coats of mail and trappings embossed in gold. The towers of Jerusalem are seen in the background and above there are angels making compassionate gestures— one of them receives the soul of the penitent thief— while on the other side a harpy fastens her claws on to his impenitent companion. In power, exuberance of imagination and fantasy of detail, it is unmatched by any other tableau except possibly that which depicted Creation. There is not a single figure in it that does not show an individual and intense reaction to the scene.

This was exactly the meaning given to the phrase
[1] ibid.

'composition of place' by Ignatius Loyola in the *Spiritual Exercises*. It was a peculiar feature of his method of prayer and a by-product of his visit to the Holy Land. Angela left her Company no such instruction, but the fact that on her second visit to Varallo she took with her two of her followers indicates that it was in this manner also that she gave them direction in prayer. 'By exercising the corporeal senses,' she wrote in her *Rule*, 'we prepare the mind for prayer';[1] and in a beautiful composition of her own, written shortly after her second visit to Varallo, and incorporated into this chapter, we perhaps get an indication of the spiritual graces which she received there in the chapel of the Crucifixion. 'Guard, O Lord, my affections and my senses that they may not stray in any and every direction, nor lead me away from the true light of thy face, the satisfaction of every afflicted heart.' Angela was not as precise as Ignatius. Were it possible to establish a connection between the two great reformers, the historian would not hesitate to see in Ignatius' writings the influence of Angela, or, according to his dating of the unformulated principles of Angela's *Rule*, the influence of Ignatius on Angela. The summary of Angela's lifelong experience in things spiritual, and the climax of her teaching on prayer, is contained in the conclusion of Chapter V of her *Rule*. Possibly it received its final formulation at Varallo, which for her appears in some ways to have occupied much the same place that Manresa did in the life of Ignatius. Nowhere in the lives of the two saints,

[1] *Rule*, ch. V.

both of them founders of religious orders that at once became engaged in the vast task of holding back the onset of heresy, are there two prayers that run so parallel in phrasing and sentiments as Ignatius's *Sume et Suscipe*, the synthesis of his *Exercises*, and Angela's prayer, 'I beseech thee, O Lord, receive all my will. Receive all my thoughts, words and deeds, all my being, interior and exterior, which I lay at the feet of thy Divine Majesty, beseeching thee that thou wouldst accept it, though so truly unworthy.' There are differences, of course. Angela's prayer, for instance, is not as provocative as Ignatius's, but both are the prayers of saints alert to the evils of their day, one an ex-soldier, the other a shrewd woman who in her own fashion and in the measure of her education, saw in complete submission to God in His Church the only way to the salvation and unity of a divided Christendom.

At the time of Angela's first visit to Varallo only a few of the chapels were completed. It seems that Bernardino Caimi's plan allowed only for the Holy Places of Jerusalem, but as the shrine became more popular, chapels were built to recall all the principal events of Our Lord's life regardless of whether they occurred in Jerusalem or not, and, later still, scenes were added from the Old Testament. Francesco Sforza was a patron of the work, and also many Milanese noblemen; and indeed, it is likely that Francesco suggested the pilgrimage to Angela, for on her return journey through Milan she was invited to stay in his palace. At this time also Charles V was contributing funds to Varallo for the work on the chapel of the Crucifixion, possibly as a token of his reconciliation with Francesco. Angela's own visit would also have helped to make the shrine more widely known, particularly in Brescia, but the greatest impetus to the work was given after Angela's death by the visits of St Charles Borromeo.

When Angela made her pilgrimages Gaudenzio Ferrari and his assistants were busy painting, both in the chapels and in the Franciscan Church of S. Maria delle Grazie below the Monte Sacro where Angela would have stayed. There were many occasions on which she would have spoken with Gaudenzio about his work which was to occupy him the greater part of his life. He was an artist of nobility and devotion. Earlier in his career at Milan he had not unnaturally fallen under the influence of Leonardo da Vinci—indeed, one of the figures done under his direction in the chapel of the Crucifixion is said to be the most accurate portrait of the artist—and he was as versatile as his Milanese master: a philosopher, mathematician, poet and musician who played well on the lyre. Angela may have heard of him earlier in Rome, where for a while he had worked under Raphael and had painted with him the *stanze* of the Vatican through which Angela would have passed on her way to her audience with Clement VII. But even during this period he was frequently at Varallo, for with many interruptions he had been decorating the chancel wall of S. Maria delle Grazie with scenes of Our Lord's life which were to be models for the Stations on the Monte Sacro; and he was gathering about him associates who would assure the completion of the work after his death. He was imaginative beyond most northern artists and had a particular gift for portraying the swift movement of his figures. On the chancel wall of S. Maria delle Grazie, with the technique he owed to his master, he drew the bystanders at the scene of the Crucifixion with a graded measure of sorrow according to their nearness to the Cross.

From 1524 until 1539 Ferrari made Varallo his home and gathered about him sculptors, artists and architects who under his direction were to create the New Jerusalem. At the same time he decorated the churches of the valley, many of its wayside chapels, and he became known to all pilgrims to Varallo. It may well have been that he inspired Angela to commission painters to adorn the walls of the first meeting-place of her Company in the cathedral square of Brescia. Angela certainly admired him greatly as a man as well as an artist, for as the Synod of Novara declared, he was as pious as he was gifted: *Gaudensus noster opera quidem eximius sed magis eximie pius.* In his own day and after it his place as an artist was exaggerated, for after Michelangelo, Raphael and Leonardo, he was reckoned the greatest painter in Italy, but he suffered from too many masters to be put in such company. Nevertheless, he was still a great artist. Here at Varallo by a combination of all the arts then practised in Italy he had discovered a form of Christian instruction through a combination of painting and sculpture that accounts in part for Angela's method of teaching.

On her return down the valley through Novara Angela stopped at Milan. For several days she was the guest of Francesco Sforza in the palace which his grandfather, Francesco I, had reconstructed on the remains of the old fortress of the Visconti. The young Francesco, who now for a brief period was enjoying the possession of his duchy, took advantage of Angela's visit to seek further advice. In his short life he had experienced every kind of frustration and sadness. Unfortunately there is no contemporary portrait of him that has survived, except one, a small masterpiece executed when he was a fat-cheeked child in exile. For this reason still further interest attaches itself to the painting by Calcinardi in Desenzano church. Though done in the early nineteenth century it may well represent a tradition, for it is known that the artist did all he could to get the factual details of his composition exact. Here Angela with her two companions in the background is shown standing, more stiffly than might be expected, in front of the Duke, a young, finely dressed yet saddened character who clearly looks to her for help. It was not their last meeting. At Cremona, where both Angela and Francesco took refuge during the following year, they would have seen each other frequently. Francesco asked Angela on this occasion to remain in the city. Angela replied as she had replied to the Pope, that she was needed in Brescia.

Before leaving Milan Angela would have visited the two popular churches close to the Sforza Palace, S. Ambrogio and the equally ancient S. Eustorgio. Less than a hundred years before, in the process of excavation, the body of St Ambrose had been recovered and now the bronzed skeleton, flanked by the remains of SS. Gervase and Protase, all wrapped in cloth of gold, lay in a specially constructed crypt below the high altar. In the twin basilica of S. Eustorgio, the third-century bishop of Milan, Angela was shown the massive stone tomb of the Magi, built by the saint to house their bones, which he had received from Constantine and carried in a chariot from Byzantium to Milan. The tomb was now empty, for Frederick Barbarossa had removed the bodies to Cologne on his invasion of Italy.

Possibly at the suggestion of Francesco or on her own initiative, Angela, when she left Milan, took the more southerly route to Brescia in order to visit a remarkable visionary, Stefana Quinzani, prioress of a convent of Dominican Tertiaries at Soncino. The most reliable biographers of Angela say that the two holy women had long discussions together and that Angela asked her guidance, presumably on the question of the formation of her Company. It is difficult to get a precise picture of Stefana, since all accounts of her are based on the same unreliable source, the *Legenda Volgare*, which has been rightly described as a mystical romance. At the time of Angela's visit she was an old lady in her seventies. She had been born near Brescia of poor family in 1457. In early childhood her parents had moved to Soncino, where she joined the Dominican convent. For the last forty years her life had been troubled by unceasing temptations, which she countered by staggering austerities, ranging from knotted ropes around her waist to perpetual hair shirts; yet with it all she was wonderfully gay. Then, for her last thirty years she was said to have slept with a stone for a pillow, in much the same way as Angela is portrayed on her sickbed by the Desenzano artist. From childhood throughout her life she had visions in which the saints and Our Lord appeared and spoke to her. At times her raptures lasted for three days. Like Osanna she was a stigmatic. Angela, who in her *Rule* warns her followers against false mystics, saw in her an authentic saint. Indeed, among all her contemporaries Stefana appears to have been the first from whom Angela received the kind of help she had been seeking so long. In turn Angela would have comforted Stefana, for she had her detractors: a woman had been known to call her a whore in the streets and there were many who laughed openly at her extraordinary experiences. With contemplation she combined action and had done remarkable work for the poor and sick in Soncino and Milan. Angela's biographers say no more than that the two saints discussed spiritual subjects together, but it is likely that Angela revealed to Stefana some of her own mystical experiences in order to receive her guidance. Though born more humbly than Angela, she moved among all classes of people and is said to have consorted with princes, among them Angela's friend, Francesco. It was probably through Francesco that the two saints met.

Stefana died within twelve months of her meeting with Angela on 2 January 1530. Among her preternatural gifts was the power of foretelling at times future events. We do not know whether Stefana gave Angela any foreknowledge of the last important decade of her own life, which was to see the foundation of her Company. On leaving Stefana, Angela returned to Brescia. There was to be one further interruption before she gave her companions the *Rule* which was to embody all the experiences of her prayer and pilgrimage.

10

Sojourn in Cremona

On her return Angela found Brescia in a greater state of disturbance than it had been since she first moved into the city from Desenzano fifteen years earlier. Charles V was making for Bologna, where he was to be crowned Emperor by Clement VII. It was feared that on his way he would lay siege to Brescia and then move on to Milan. His forces were scattered over north Italy, lawless, plundering, half-organized units. There was a general flight south from Brescia to Cremona. At such a time it was impossible for Angela to take any steps towards the foundation of the new Order she had discussed with Stefana Quinzani. All the conditions were present for the work except peace. The Patengola family had already left for Cremona. Agostino Gallo, a leading citizen who was to have an important influence on the last years of Angela's life, followed. Then, as the Imperial troops surrounded Brescia, the remaining families of position left the city. Francesco Sforza, aware of the futility of defending Milan against the Emperor, moved his entire court to Cremona.

After all the citizens who could help her in the foundation of her Company had left, Angela was finally persuaded to join them. Moreover, she was now sick— indeed, shortly afterwards she was thought to be dying —and in her condition there was little she could do to relieve the sufferings of the citizens. On the other hand, at Cremona it was still possible that she might found her Company. All who were likely to join it were already there.

Angela's friend, Agostino Gallo, who had already established himself at Cremona, was a wealthy patron of artists, a lover of music and country life as well as a benevolent landlord who was constantly introducing into his own and his friends' estates new methods of land improvement and new theories of flax-growing and the cultivation of vines.[1] For many years he and Angela had known each other. After Angela's death he testified to his long friendship with her, perhaps exaggerating his dependence on her. 'Not only I myself did not know how to live without her,' he wrote, 'but my wife and my family were the same, and certainly my sister Hippolyta also.' During her married life Hippolyta was very intimate with Angela and even more so after her husband died in 1528.

During this period of trouble Agostino and his widowed sister had rented a house in Cremona in the Via S. Vittore on the outskirts of the city, a fashionable and newly built street off the road that led out of

[1] Agostino Gallo (1499–1570) of Brescia has been described as the leading agronomist of his age and the father of Italian agriculture. His book, *Le venti giornate dell' agricoltura et de' piaceri della villa*, a treatise on agriculture written in dialogue form and based on his own studies and experiments, first appeared in 1550. It went through more than twenty Italian editions and has also been translated into French. (Michaud, *Biographie Universelle*, XV, p. 458.)

Cremona to Mantua. There is no trace today of this house, for one side of the street has been rebuilt and the other altogether demolished. Nor does anything remain of the church of S. Vittore at the junction of this street and the Via Assellina, where Angela would have attended Mass. Only the arched colonnade, which formed part of the cloister, stands now at the entrance to a small unattractive block of tenement houses to indicate that a church formerly stood on the site. To judge from a plan of the city drawn in the year 1645, the church of S. Vittore, after the cathedral and St. Agatha's, would appear to have been one of the most important and ancient places of worship in Cremona.[1] In the year that Angela lived there it was still a Benedictine monastery, though a few years after her return to Brescia it was handed over to the Servite Friars.[2]

Agostino Gallo and his sister had the same affection for Angela that characterized Caterina Patengola in the days when Angela was still working in Desenzano. The admiration in which they both held her led them not unnaturally to notice the smallest details in her behaviour. 'She lived most harshly, suffering the intense heat or extreme cold,' says Agostino, testifying to her life in the Via S. Vittore. 'And she deprived herself of all comfort in sleep, since what little she actually had,

[1] cf. map of the city entitled *Cremona Fidelissima Citta* in the municipal library, Cremona.

[2] The church remained in the hands of the Servites until it was suppressed in 1798. In 1871 the Via S. Vittore was renamed *Largo Paolo Sarpi*.

she took on a mat without coverings and on a piece of wood; and in such a way that before daybreak she rolled the mat up and there was no other bed to be seen.' And as he continues, his curiosity peers through his statement: 'Nor did I see any kind of vessel for wine. I noticed that she drank nothing but water; with this exception, that on the feasts of the Nativity of Our Lord and the Resurrection she had a single thumb measure of wine at dinner. Always she took a little bread and also fruit and vegetables, but very parsimoniously.'

In this brief sketch Angela can be seen struggling to keep her privacy. The accommodation that Gallo could offer her did not protect her from the prying eyes of her host. There is something more restrained in Antonio Romano's statement. Both in temperament and in approach these two friends were as far removed from one another as two natives of the same city could be. Antonio, a self-controlled, phlegmatic, loyal, considerate man, is so strikingly different from Agostino Gallo that the contrast comes through the evidence they give. There can be little doubt that Angela was less happy in Gallo's house and company, and that she found him perhaps a pious and flamboyant extrovert, too boastful of his friendship with her. At the same time the appreciation that she showed them both says much about her character. She lived in Romano's house for fourteen years, whereas she was hardly fourteen months with Gallo both in Brescia and Cremona.

With her reputation established throughout northern

Italy as an adviser and comforter of both men and women, Angela, after a few weeks in Cremona, became the most sought-after person in the city. Apart from all the influential citizens of Brescia who were living there in exile, the people of Cremona now came to see her as her name became known among them. Owing to the alarms of war many of her visitors were in a state of excitement that wore down her health. Probably without exaggeration Agostino Gallo says that 'from morning until night she was beset by people of all conditions; by numbers of religious and pious people, as well as by gentlemen and ladies and other folk both from Cremona and Milan'. And he adds, echoing the Scriptures, 'Everyone of them marvelled at the wisdom they found in her, and it was clear that she was converting many of them and making them change their lives.'

Under this excessive strain she became gravely ill— until now her country constitution had stood her well, for it is the first illness in her life that is recorded—and for several days she lay apparently on the point of death.

Among the subjects chosen by the Desenzano artist to illustrate the critical phases in Angela's career is the composition that shows her stretched at length on the floor of her room in Gallo's house in the Via S. Vittore in momentary expectation of death. Angela is seen here in the surroundings described by Gallo. The square room is bare except for a wooden table and two chairs. On the table are a crucifix, a breviary and a quill resting in an inkpot, as though on the day she was taken ill Angela was working in prayer on the *Rule* of her Company. A single framed picture of Our Lady and the Child hangs on the otherwise bare walls. Resting on a chair set close to her wooden pillow is a half-filled glass of water. A bright light entering through the window spreads out in rays to cover her body from head to foot. She is tranquil but ashen, clothed in the habit and head-dress of a Franciscan Tertiary.

The picture tries to catch the moment when Angela's life had been abandoned by the physicians of Cremona. As news of her condition spread through the city, many came to see here, as they thought, for the last time. Propped up on her wooden pillow, she began to speak with great animation (her words are not recorded) and then she fell into a rapture that lasted half an hour. Agostino Gallo continues the strange story. 'She raised herself into a sitting position and talked with fervour of the joy of heaven for thirty minutes; her face was resplendent, so that all who crowded into the room thought they were in heaven.' Suddenly she recovered her physical strength and knew she was cured of her illness. Gerolamo Patengola was there. Angela turned to him and complained that he had told her she was dying merely to tease her. Gerolamo protested that he was convinced that she was going to die before that day had fully dawned.

A few other details are added. Angela called for her habit and veil. 'Living and dying,' she said with Franciscan simplicity, 'let us bless the Providence of God.' She considered that her sins had held her back from death. 'Jesus Christ gained that happiness only at the price of fatigue and suffering, but I scarcely know yet what it is to suffer.'

In connection with this illness a well-authenticated incident is told that illustrates the humour of Gerolamo and his simple faith. As Angela lay sick he composed her epitaph in rhyming verses. Their meaning is this:

> Within this Tomb lies Buried one whose Name
> Angelic Deeds and Words to all Proclaim,
> Who dwelt in Silence, in her Cell apart,
> True Peace to cherish in her Virgin Heart.
> God's Child she was, Obedient and Devout,
> The Foe of All that kept her Master out.
> In Heaven now she Lives, among the Blest,
> A Crown of Palms upon her head, At Rest.[1]

Gerolamo, taking pride in his schoolboy composition, took out his verses, explaining to Angela that he proposed to inscribe them on her tomb. The room was filled with friends awaiting her last struggle. Gerolamo, snatching at this moment, showered on her the praise that she had always declined in her life; and bad though his verses are, they indicate nevertheless the kind of veneration in which Angela was held.

[1] Quella ch'el nome, l'opre e la favella
D' Angela tenne, qui sepolta giace:
Vergine visse in taciturna cella,
Godendo ivi la vera interna pace:
Di Dio diletta et obbediente ancella
Nimica fu di cio che al senso piace.
Hor vive lieta in cielo coronata
Di palme il crin fra gli Angeli beata.

At this time Francesco Sforza was in Cremona. Again he had rightly determined that it was useless for him to offer resistance unaided to the overwhelming forces of the Emperor. Three years earlier, for five months, he had bravely withstood him in his castle in Milan until he was starved into surrender. Cremona was the obvious refuge for him in exile. He had settled here four years earlier, when he was at odds with the Emperor and had first sought Angela's advice. Moreover, he had other ties with the city. About one and a half miles from its centre, on the road to Mantua, Francesco's grandfather, Francesco Sforza I, had built the simple but magnificent church of S. Sigismondo, to celebrate his wedding in 1441 to Bianca Maria Visconti. The building was not begun until 1483 and the work of decoration was still going on during Angela's stay in Cremona. Possibly with Francesco and with the artists who were at work on the six side chapels, she discussed the subjects they chose for the frescoes. This was certainly a matter on which the Duke would have taken Angela's advice. In the cloister attached to the church—its immense simplicity and harmony stood in stark contrast to all the cloisters of the old city churches—Angela would have found rest away from her persistent callers, many of whom, as Gallo relates, came from the Duke's suite.

Francesco did not live there, but probably in the Trecchi Palace, in the Via Trecchi, opposite the porticoed church of St Agatha, the most externally attractive though not the most interesting church in Cremona. There is a record that Francesco established his Court here in 1526; and it is likely that he did so again in the winter of 1530, which he and Angela both spent at Cremona. Even in its restored condition it is one of the finest buildings in the city. There Angela and the Duke would have met, and held their long unrecorded conversations. The young Duke, whose short, sad life was the contradiction of all that is popularly believed of a Renaissance prince, was destined to die before Angela. In this year he was still only thirty-five. Three years later Charles V imposed on him a bride, Christina of Denmark, a niece of his and a child of thirteen. At the time, the bridegroom, Angela's friend, was a broken man of thirty-eight, an invalid, grey-haired, walking with the aid of a stick, and at times deprived of the use of his limbs. His only comfort was in the love his people had for him. He died childless after two years of marriage. With him the ruling house of Milan died. The widowed Christina, aged fifteen, was then wooed by Henry VIII of England, who, anxious to be informed of the girl's charms, commissioned Holbein to paint her portrait, which now hangs in the National Gallery. Possibly in the archives of the Duchy of Milan or in the other archives of northern Italian towns, later writers on St Angela will uncover the full story of Angela's relations with this most tragic and beloved Italian prince.

On 24 February 1530, Charles V was crowned by Clement VII in Bologna; peace was restored and Francesco Sforza reinstated in Milan. Angela, with her friends, returned to Brescia.

On her return, in the spring of 1530, Angela lived in the house of Agostino Gallo. This was a temporary residence. No reason is suggested by her biographers for her departure from Antonio Romano's house near St Agatha's. But her stay with Gallo was very short; Angela clearly was intensely occupied with the foundation of her Company. She was now fifty-six. By the reckoning of her day she was an old lady. The one thing she needed now for the work to which all her prayer and experience had led was independence in her movements and uninterrupted prayer. Possibly some simple reason, such as the destruction of Romano's house during the troubles in Brescia, may explain why Angela transferred her domicile to Gallo's house; but more probably, after the hospitality she had received at Cremona, she felt obliged to accept Gallo's invitation to live with him.

Curiously it is not Angela's stay in this house, but Agostino Gallo's own occupation of it that is today commemorated by an engraved plaque on the right side of the entrance. It reads: *Agostino Gallo qui ebbe sua casa ma predilesse la villa i cui benefizi e diletti celebro con utili insegnamenti nel libro le venti giornati dell' agricoltura 1499–1570.*[1] Inside the house has been reconstructed: only its façade remains directly facing the fine church of S. Clemente across a small piazza. It was the time that Moretto, the most prolific and, with Gerolamo Roma-

---

[1] Agostino Gallo lived in this house, but he preferred his villa, and made known its pleasures and comforts in the book which contains useful instruction *Le venti giornati dell' agricoltura.*

nino, the greatest of the native Brescian artists, was decorating this church, where he later chose to be buried. There, among his finest series of paintings, behind the altars of the church, is a large canvas of St Ursula which portrays her with two banners. Art historians date the painting in the very year, namely 1530, that Angela was living opposite the church: and as Gallo was the most renowned patron of the artists, it can be taken for certain that Moretto and Angela met in his house and discussed the subject of this picture. It is perhaps not fanciful to suggest that Angela herself might have provided Moretto with his model, for the Ursula of the Moretto is a woman of Angela's age. Angela was now gathering about her ladies of a younger generation who were to form the nucleus of her Order. The companions of St Ursula, painted with their fair complexion are certainly Brescian types. It was one of Moretto's finest paintings, but after several restorations it has lost a great deal of its grandeur.

Angela remained in Gallo's house only a few months after her return. Here she completed her recovery in health. The doctors who attended her, as Gallo testified, were amazed to see how she 'had developed quite a different constitution from other people and how the medicines others took for a cure by purging were absorbed by her as food'; but he adds that, in order not to be thought singular, she obediently allowed the physicians to prescribe medicines though they did her no good. 'More often she would get better simply by eating onions, leeks and other vegetables which suited her constitution better; and if she continued unwell, she would cure herself by washing her head.'

Although, as has been said, Agostino Gallo lived only across the street from S. Clemente, neither his house nor the church gave Angela the privacy she wanted. In the same year that she returned from Cremona, she moved to a room in a house adjoining the church of St Barnabas. No reason is given for the choice of this place, which is not connected with the name of any Brescian family. It would seem that she had determined now to live alone in order to work freely towards the foundation of her Company. It is possible that the room may have been given to her through the influence of Francesco Sforza, who had stayed at the convent attached to the church during his visit to Brescia. It was during the time she lived there that she made her second visit to Varallo.

11

S. Afra's

The church of St Barnabas lies between S. Clemente and S. Afra. For eighteen months Angela lived in a small house next to the church; then she made the last move of her life.

In every house in Brescia where she found new living quarters, from her first day in Brescia to her last, she lived alongside a church. In this way she was able to pray more easily during both day and night, unnoticed by her friends. Although her biographers speak only of her vigils in the crypt of S. Afra's during her last eight years, it is almost certain that night prayer was the habit of her lifetime. The fact that these vigils are not recorded in earlier years or in other churches is no argument, in such a scantily documented life, that it was not a habit formed in her first days in Brescia or earlier at Salo and Grezze, where she followed, with the more literal interpretation of a child, in the footsteps of the saints.

Her stay at St Barnabas's was the shortest of all, if we except the few months she passed in Gallo's house. Angela was clearly anxious to be independent. Gallo's house, opposite S. Clemente, with its constant throng of distinguished guests, did not give Angela the solitude she sought. Moreover, it would seem that Agostino Gallo, like Caterina Patengola fifteen years earlier, was trying to dominate Angela's life: his affection would seem to have been too possessive. Indeed, Agostino himself testified that he 'became her prisoner at once', after he got to know her well at Cremona, and 'was unable to live without her'. Angela, however, was from the beginning determined to found her Company in complete detachment from her friends, no matter how helpful or useful they had been.

The example of her life had prepared the way for the foundation. For many years now women and young girls had been visiting her without constraint, attracted both by her calmness and strength of character. Often they had expressed their wish to work under her direction, but hitherto she had encouraged each individually in whatever task she was most fitted to do. At the same time much was lost through lack of organization.

In the vision at Brudazzo she had seen the maidens in compact companies, each company escorted by an angel, and the memory of the vision was always with her. It was at this time, during her brief stay near the church of St Barnabas, before the formal foundation of her Company, that the first groups took shape; and it was with one of these groups that she made her second pilgrimage to Varallo. Now that she was known to all in Brescia and her reputation fortuitously enhanced after her astonishing recovery of health at Cremona, she was in a unique position to introduce to one another all the Brescian ladies who were anxious to help in relief of the sick and the victims of war. She was able to arrange for them to meet together, and without demanding any change in their external way of life, she gave them the spiritual inspiration they needed to persevere in their work. And it was with the purpose of training more carefully a handful of her followers, who were to become leaders in her Company, that she took ten of them to Varallo on her second pilgrimage. The Preamble to the *Rule* had perhaps already been written: and it contains a suppressed allusion to the bands of virgins she saw at Brudazzo and also to her own spiritual experiences and journeys: 'Observe the *Rule* as the road you are to travel . . . that we may surmount all the perils and difficulties. The angels and celestial choirs shall be with us always, since we participate in the Angelic life.'

And it is interesting also that at the very beginning of this introduction Angela should insist on perseverance, as though she had experienced more than once the falling away of early companions. She insists that all who enter must seize on 'every way and means necessary to the end. No good beginning is sufficient in itself without perseverance'.

Perhaps for this reason she bided her time until she had around her many admirers of a younger generation than her own. Several of them were no more than girls. The attraction of her character for the young was as great as for her elders and those of her own years. In a paragraph in her *Rule* concerning the age of candidates to be admitted to the Company she faced with sound sense the problem of the young applicant: 'She must be at least twelve years old when she presents herself, fifteen when she is invested and taken into the Chapter, and eighteen or twenty when she is inscribed in the authentic register.' And here Angela adds a phrase concerning youthful aspirants that gives one of the few indications in the whole of the primitive *Rule* that the Company was to be engaged primarily in the education of the young. 'Let it be remembered', she says, 'that those of minor age may be admitted solely for the purpose of teaching them the ways of the Company.'

This is perhaps the most pregnant sentence in the *Rule*, and it is proof that at least during the last years of her life, if not for a long time before this, Angela herself was engaged in the spiritual formation of the young. From this activity developed the largest and most important educational system for girls in the post-Tridentine Church that was to run parallel with the work of the Society of Jesus in the education of young men.

Every word in the first paragraph of the first section of the *Rule* is carefully meditated. Little is known about the actual composition of the document: but on internal evidence it would seem that it was written, not as a single fully developed charter, but in sections composed at long intervals, perhaps of several years, as her activity and horizon expanded. The earlier chapters embody a wider experience than the later ones, and were probably conceived and tested by practice long before they were written. Certainly at the time Angela was living at St Barnabas's the first chapters were already the law of her followers. Probably on her move to S. Afra's they were formulated in paragraphs and the whole work was systematized.

At no time did Angela have any idea of forming a new

enclosed Order. Already in Brescia there were too many
religious houses of nuns for the number of girls that had
an authentic vocation to the contemplative life. Scandals
and lax discipline were common, and indeed inevitable,
as long as custom allowed parents to force into these
convents their younger daughters who had no chance of
marriage and to covenant for their acceptance by the
provision of modest dowries by which all such houses
were maintained. In this way also parents were able to
provide more handsome allowances for their elder or
more attractive children and marry them into important
families. Angela's reaction to these abuses can be seen in
the first chapters of her *Rule*, where she insists on complete freedom of choice in all who wished to join her
Company and a disinterested purpose to serve God. In
this her observation had been the same as Ignatius', and
her remedies similar. 'With a firm intention to serve God
in this kind of life,' writes Angela, 'the applicant must
enter gladly and of her own free will.' And moreover,
she must undergo a long period of testing before she is
finally admitted.

Already the companions she took with her to Varallo
had been through this period of testing: and she had in
them a nucleus of followers whom she knew intimately.

It is clear that Angela left Gallo's house for St Barnabas's in order to be unimpeded in her work. Now
within a few months, immediately after her return from
Varallo, she made the most significant move of her life,
to an apartment next to the church of the Canons of the
Lateran at S. Afra. There the Company was officially

founded and formally approved by the Bishop of Brescia.

In her emphasis on a true vocation, Angela was a reformer; and, at the same time, in her conception of religious life without the cloister, she was an innovator. Her followers were to be in the world, but with a calling that made them, in her simple and evocative words, more estimable than 'empresses, queens, duchesses and the like'. And while she herself wore the Franciscan habit, she did not prescribe it for others. However, she made recommendations in the matter of dress which have a quaint and antiquarian interest today. She lays down that their costume should be simple. All should attend to its careful arrangement and wear their bodices properly fastened, and not half-fastened in the fashion affected by Brescian ladies of the day; all, too, should 'wear a veil of linen, not too fine and transparent'.[1]

In her insistence that her followers should not ape the fashions of her day, but should be dressed becomingly, Angela gives an illuminating commentary on Brescian costume of her time. She was determined that the good works of her followers should, as far as possible, be hidden both from themselves and from their friends, and that on no account were they to attract attention to themselves by any extreme of fashion. There is need only to read the letters of the Brescian lady, Laura Cereta, to see the good sense of Angela's recommendations. 'One

[1] Later in the century St Charles Borromeo, who revised the *Rule* and added sections to it, made their veil and a leather cincture the 'proper habit' of the Order.

lady', writes Laura Cereta, 'has a veritable tower of false hair on her head, another drapes herself in great tresses of false hair down her shoulders; some have one necklace on their breast and a second one hanging from their arm, while some also have their throat tied round with a mesh of pearls.' Thus weddings became shows, and dress the entry into society. If ladies of the upper classes were to seek admission into Angela's Company, then they had to fall in with her simple way of life. They were to have 'no ruffles, plaits or frills on the chemise' and wear no 'novelties nor transparent materials and other vanities' that could 'sully their conscience' and give scandal to others. Their slippers and sandals, as well as their shoes, were to be black, simple and modest.

It would seem that she had difficulty in insisting on these prescriptions, for in her *Counsels*, which are of later date than the *Rule*, she again exhorts young aspirants not to become attached to the vanity of attractive head-dresses.

Under Venetian influence all the wealthier citizens had adorned their houses with balconies, which even today give a special attraction to many old streets in the central section of the city. Here young ladies would attract the attention of passing gallants; but Angela did not feel it necessary to do more than warn her followers in the most general terms against the practice of the day: she cautions them simply 'for many reasons' to avoid 'loitering on the balconies, at doorways and in the streets, whether they are alone or accompanied,' and advises them against going to weddings, to balls, jousts and other spectacles. In this same section, also, Angela unwittingly draws a picture of herself walking from house to house on her errands of charity in the crowded and noisy streets of Brescia. 'Going along the road,' she tells her followers, 'walk with eyes cast down . . . and go quickly, not delaying, nor stopping here and there along the way, standing to gaze curiously at anything' or stopping to 'listen to the addresses of men'.

In these few simple lines Angela drew a picture of the first unenclosed religious sisters walking briskly on their business through crowded streets—a picture that was a novelty in her own day, but has now become part of the city scene throughout the world. The rules she laid down for her own Company have become the distinguishing mark of all unenclosed nuns from her day to ours.

It was at this time, during her stay at Varallo, that the bonds that united her first companions were formed. At this critical moment in her life two events occurred to speed her in her work of forming other small groups and bringing them together in a single Company. At Brudazzo the virgins had appeared to her in just similar groups. She had carried out thus far the instructions of the voice she then heard, but it was a further step, perhaps not so plainly indicated to her in prayer, towards the foundation of her Company. That the memory of Brudazzo was especially with her at this time is clear from the sentence that stands at the head of the first chapter of the *Rule*: 'Let it be remembered first of all that anyone who desires to enter or to be admitted into this Company must be a virgin.' The phrase, 'it must be remembered', can hardly be explained unless Angela is evoking her own vision.

The first critical event during her stay at St Barnabas's was her meeting with Fra Serafino. He was a Bolognese, who had joined the Canons of the Lateran and was resident at Brescia at the church of S. Afra. He is the first of Angela's confessors whom we know by name, a deeply spiritual and wise priest who became her director at this most important period of her life; and he appears also to have been a man of influence both in his own Order and in the city. More than any other individual priest he helped Angela both in practical and in spiritual problems. It was he who arranged for her to leave St Barnabas's and to live in a larger room attached to the canonry buildings, and he became also the first spiritual director of her companions The right accommodation and the right director, therefore, were given to Angela at the same time, and perhaps also the right bishop.

Among the reasons for Angela's delay in founding her Company may have been the attitude of Paolo Zane, the old Bishop of Brescia, though it may be no more than a coincidence that he died on 12 March 1531 in the year Angela's groups of ladies took on recognizable form as a confraternity.

Zane had been Bishop of Brescia from the time Angela was seven years old. He was a Venetian, a nephew or cousin of his predecessor, Bishop Laurentio Zane, who gave him the See when he was a young man of twenty-two, on condition that he did not succeed until he had reached his twenty-eighth year. The transaction was confirmed by the Pope. Paolo took over the administration of the see in 1481. When Angela came to Brescia from Desenzano he had already been bishop thirty-five years. Not enough is known of him to be able to assess what his attitude to Angela would have been; but it is recorded that he was devout to Our Blessed Lady and added yet another church to the city, S. Maria delle Grazie, and contributed to its building out of his personal fortune. In politics he is likely to have sided with the French against the Spanish faction. It is known that he supported with enthusiasm the enterprise of the Contessa Laura Gambara, a French lady married to a Brescian nobleman, who with his help built and endowed a house for penitent women near the church of St Denis. There may be significance in the fact that Angela began to organize her followers into a Company only in the months following his death. He was then seventy years old and had possessed the See for fifty-eight years.[1]

It was only at the end of the year that a successor was appointed, Cardinal Francesco Cornaro, who had already been a power in the papal court for many years before the election of Clement VII. He was the third cardinal in his generation, Venetians of a leading Senatorial family, and related to Caterina Cornaro, Queen of Cyprus. It was unusual for a man with such connections and influence at the papal court to be transferred to a northern See of secondary importance. But besides being

[1] F. Ughelli, *Italia Sacra*, pp. 760–2.

a man of reforming zeal and a high sense of responsibility, he had the reputation of a peacemaker on an international scale, and it may have been Clement's intention to place one of his most skilled negotiators in a part of Italy that during his lifetime had been the cause of constant warfare. Moreover, he was an avowed friend of the Emperor Charles, and was one of his three favoured candidates for the Papacy on the death of Clement VII in 1534.

Cardinal Cornaro entered Brescia at the end of 1531, a 'herald of peace, riding a Turkish horse, covered with damask, in beautiful procession such as they have at Corpus Christi. He dismounted in the centre of the Cathedral Square and there blessed his new people.'[1] It was under the new bishop that Angela was to get ecclesiastical approval for her Company.

[1] Rossi, *Uomini Illustri da Brescia.*

12

The Foundation of the Company

Although Angela continued to live in the two rooms at S. Afra's put at her disposal by the Canons, the larger room in which she had held the first meeting of her companions soon became insufficient for her needs. Twelve months later she accepted the offer of a meeting-place in the house of her widowed friend, Elizabeth Prato, in the Piazza del Duomo in the centre of the city. Here, towards the end of 1534, Angela began to hold something like regular gatherings of her companions, and at their request to give them spiritual conferences. Rightly, this house, which was demolished at the end of the eighteenth century, was regarded as the first oratory of the Ursulines.

From the time Angela left St Barnabas's church for S. Afra's her fame as a saint grew rapidly: so much so that during the last eight years of her life she appears already to have been canonized by the citizens of Brescia. Stories were told of her works of charity and peace-making, of her night vigils and penances; and there were many witnesses to her astonishing knowledge of Scripture, which was considered more divine than human. 'Although she had never been taught the alphabet,' writes Agostino Gallo, 'she was often seen reading religious books, and frequently when she was visited by priests and religious, and particularly by preachers and theologians, who were anxious to get her clarification of the psalms, or prophets or apocalypse, or some book of the Old or New Testament, they listened to her explanations with amazement.' But her popular esteem was most enhanced at this time by an unusual grace that was given her while she was attending Mass in the church of St Barnabas. No exact date is given for the incident, but it belongs to her first days of residence at S. Afra's. Tales of the special favours granted to her in prayer had been current for many years, but Angela herself discounted them in conversation, in which her stress was always on solid and unostentatious Christian virtue. But in prayer this morning at St Barnabas's she was seen by a large congregation raised from the ground. There were many witnesses, and it was exactly the kind of incident that in popular imagination set the seal on her sanctity and accounted in part at least for the astonishing progress she made in her work during the last years of her life.

The story is well authenticated, and was told on oath by a Brescian citizen, Bertolino Boscoloni. 'It might have been thirty-four years ago if I remember correctly', Bertolino testified,[1] 'that Sister Angela lived in a house near S. Afra's below the fountain where I sometimes went to see her, for she was held in great esteem on account of her spiritual life and I was her neighbour. One day I found myself in the church of St Barnabas nearby hearing Mass at the altar of St Nicholas of Tolentino. At that Mass I saw Sister Angela present with a large

[1] Boscoloni gave his testimony on 21 June 1567. This would place the phenomenon in the year 1533.

number of people. While the priest was reading the Gospel, I and many others there also saw Sister Angela, who was then standing, raised up from the ground a span's length, as though she were suspended in a marvellous way. To me it seemed a miraculous event.'

By a span Bertolino meant the width of a hand. He remembered the time, place and the detail, and appears to have been impressed by the fact that the levitation occurred not while Angela was kneeling at a more solemn moment of the Mass but when she was standing during the reading of the Gospel. The picture of St Nicholas that hung above the altar where Angela was at Mass is now in the civic museum of Brescia, for the church is no longer in use, but is now converted to secular purposes.

Bertolino's final sentence confirms the suggestion that this was the first time Angela had been seen by a group of people raised from the ground in prayer, and that the incident attracted much public attention to her. 'It became known to the citizens everywhere,' he says, 'and they came to appreciate her holiness and her religious life.' In itself it was only one of many external graces that Angela was granted, but the publicity attaching to it, though utterly unsought, added to her popular reputation for holiness in her last years of work.[1]

[1] Levitation of the body in prayer has no necessary connection with ecstasy; it is a distinct gift and it is explained as an imperfect participation in the gift of fleetness, which will be bestowed on glorified bodies. cf. Poulain, *Graces of Interior Prayer*, pp. 550 et seq.

Today not even the site of Elizabeth Prato's house can be identified. When it was demolished no attempt was made to preserve the paintings that decorated the walls of the meeting-room. In commissioning the paintings, Angela was following the Franciscan tradition of her day. Possibly they were the work of Moretto or Romanino, the leading Brescian artists, but there is no record of this. Although a description of the paintings has survived, no attribution has ever been made. Significantly they were begun and finished in 1534, the very year that Angela occupied the room.

It is possible also that Gaudenzio Ferrari came from Varallo for the work after her second visit to the shrine. Angela had been impressed by his painting, and particularly by his treatment of the theme of the Passion, which was the central mystery of her own devotional life. On the wall above the altar in Elizabeth Prato's room was a Crucifixion scene. Below the figure of Our Lord on the Cross knelt Our Lady, St John and the holy women. It is as though Angela was placing her first companions with them at the foot of the Cross, where they would be given the humility and strength needed to combat heresy. The remaining walls were covered with an upper and lower series of paintings. Above were scenes of Our Lord's life, much in the same style, it would seem, as on the chancel arch of the church of S. Maria delle Grazie at Varallo. The lower series represented the Assumption of Our Lady and a most significant group of saints, St Ursula on shipboard, St Afra, St Elizabeth of Hungary serving her ladies seated at table,

St Paula and her daughter, and the two early Brescian martyrs, Faustino and Giovita. Unfortunately no copies or prints were made of these paintings before they were destroyed, and it is impossible to say why Angela should have selected this particular episode in St Ursula's life.

The choice of Paula is particularly significant. It was Angela's intention to make her a secondary patron of the Company. While Ursula was the pattern and patroness of virgins, Paula was the patroness of widows. Her story, as much as the legend of St Ursula, explains the workings of Angela's mind at this time. Paula was a figure of flesh and blood, a strong-minded widow, a Roman friend of Jerome, a patron of the poor and distressed people of Rome. During her pilgrimage to Rome and possibly earlier in Palestine, where she had visited her tomb, Angela had become familiar with her story and was attracted to her, not only by her character, but because her life was passed among men who had known the early martyrs to whom she had such devotion. Paula's ancestry was legendary, for she claimed descent through the Scipios from Aeneas; she was rich and talented, and was the fitting model for the wealthy and well-born widowed ladies of Brescia who were anxious to join the Company. Like them, Paula in her married years had found some measure of worldliness inseparable from her social position, and it was only at the age of thirty-two, after the death of her husband, that she began an ascetical life that in all external details resembled Angela's own practices: she took no wine but only simple food, cared for the destitute, slept on the floor, and gave many hours to the study of Scripture. There can be little doubt that in Angela's mind Paula was the model that she desired the widowed applicants to the Company to follow, for Paula's difficulties in following God's call so closely resembled those of her Brescian friends, like the widowed Hippolyta Gallo, who were to join the Company. Moreover, Paula had left Rome to live in Nazareth and this was yet another feature that would have endeared her to Angela.

The third woman saint, Elizabeth of Hungary, whose painting was made under Angela's direction, completes the insight into Angela's mind at the time of the foundation of the Company, for Elizabeth's life after her bereavement was spent in the care of the sick, in austerity and night vigils, in good works of all kinds. Like Angela, the great devotion of her life was to the Passion of Our Lord. Still at this time her tomb at Marburg was a famed European place of pilgrimage, although, a few months before Angela's death, the Protestant Landgrave of Hesse removed her remains to a place that has never since been discovered.

Thus Ursula, Paula and Elizabeth were her chosen patronesses, along with her own martyrs of Brescia. All were saints who had experience of the world and whose apostolate lay first among their fellow-citizens. Perhaps not any one of them alone fulfilled the ideal that Angela conceived for the Company, but each contributed to the spirit she was anxious to instil in her daughters. It would be misleading to discuss Angela's choice of St Ursula without bearing in mind also the significance of the secondary patrons represented in these paintings which were made on her instructions in the very months during which she was finally to establish her Company.

In this room Angela's Company was finally established in 1534, not on 21 October, the feast of St Ursula, but on 25 November, the tenth anniversary of her return to Brescia from the Holy Land. But she chose the day, not for this reason, but because it was the feast of St Catherine of Alexandria, a virgin and martyr like St Ursula. The patroness of maidens and women students, of preachers and apologists, her feast at this time was kept with great solemnity in Italy. Cyprus claimed her as a native of the island; her tomb was on Mount Sinai, and it is likely that Angela, during her visit to the Holy Land, became familiar with every detail of her brave defence of the faith. It was the kind of feast day she might be expected to choose.

The *Rule* was not yet written, but its principles were already developed and were promulgated on this occasion. As will be seen, it was the first *Rule* drawn up for women by a woman in the Western Church. Every short chapter was to be based on her lifelong experience in dealing with the ladies for whom it was designed. No single influence predominated. In its spiritual premisses it showed dependence on the early Rule of the Third Order of St Francis; its practical tenets were an elaboration of her own approach to the spiritual difficulties that faced her in the instruction of her companions; the vision of Brudazzo inspired the Preamble to the *Rule* and, in an equal measure, the personal love of Our Lord that she deepened in Jerusalem and at Varallo. Here and there were certain lessons learned from her conversations with Stephana Quinzani and Fra Serafino. But in no sense was it to be a compilation. It can best be described as a very personal and practical expression of the spirit of a woman who, dependent only on God, had spent a lifetime in fashioning an original plan to meet the needs of the contemporary Church. Only in the context of her age can the full impact of her innovation be appreciated.

Angela was neither an intellectual nor a savant; there is no similarity between her and St Teresa of Avila or St Francis de Sales. It was her genius to translate into a code of life the reactions of her soul to the crisis in the Church in her day. While her experience of the world was limited mainly to Brescia, yet Brescia was a large enough city to be a type not only of other Italian cities, but of a greater part of northern Europe. The genius of her *Rule*, its adaptability and combination of adherence to tradition with revolutionary ideas, will be discussed later. Before her death the first draft went through emendations: what happened to it after her death belongs more to the history of her Order than to the story of its foundress.

In the room in Elizabeth Prato's house, in the Piazza del Duomo, Angela gathered her companions for prayer and for spiritual conferences. Their meetings constituted an informal noviceship, and at the same time they gave Angela an opportunity to assess the qualities of her novices so that later she was able to select from them the future Governors of the Company.

As her secretary she appointed Gabriel Cozzano, a canon attached to the Curia of the Cardinal Bishop. Angela respected him greatly for his wisdom and in her last years depended increasingly on him. It is possible that Cozzano was among the personal staff that Cardinal Cornaro had brought with him from Rome—indeed, his later role in the Company would suggest this. Anyhow it was to him, at intervals in prayer, that she dictated her *Rule*, and from that time forward Cozzano was her constant companion and confidant. With him she discussed every section, and in her last days dictated to him also her *Counsels* and her *Testament*. Indeed, Gabriel occupied during Angela's short career as foundress a position similar to that of Father Polanco in the life of St Ignatius as first General of the Society of Jesus. He was Angela's counsellor, and after her death the interpreter of her intentions. Unlike Polanco he held the post of Director of the Company, but the real strength of his position lay in his intimate knowledge of Angela's wishes, and in his quiet efficiency and self-effacement. It is difficult, in fact, to discern any outstanding characteristics of Cozzano, but it is clear from the history of Angela's last years that he was held in great regard by her companions, who respected him both for his virtue and for the confidence that their wise foundress chose to place in him. From the historian's point of view it is a pity that he was Angela's confessor and confidant and thus unable to speak freely about Angela's life, for there was no person who was better placed to give testimony to her sanctity. Only Cozzano knew the secret of her choice of St Ursula as patroness. 'It was not by mere chance that Angela gave her Company the name of Ursula. It came from heaven.' More than this he could not say. With Cozzano died the secret that all her biographers have tried to probe.

Angela's choice of such a secretary speaks much of her own character. She was anxious to reveal to none save to her director the help she had received in prayer during the composition of the *Rule*, and at the same time she wanted to submit her ideas to the criticism and advice of a priest of experience. In Cozzano she found both director and counsellor, who moreover represented for her the authority of the bishop. As a Curial official and a canonist he was in a position to work with Angela on a statement of the *Rule* of her Company in a form that would be acceptable to the bishop. As will be seen, he continued his good offices after the first foundation.

It is typical of the confidence Angela had in her vocation that she sought advice from none of the ladies, not even Barbara Fontana, with whom she shared her living quarters: so that no one more than any other should claim after her death the right of interpreting her mind. Moreover, in choosing Gabriel Cozzano as her secretary she was securing the future of her work by placing it under the guidance of an ecclesiastical authority who was likely to outlive her. Cozzano himself states modestly that he was no more than Angela's guide. The *Rule*, he testified, was her own. 'Out of humility she

wanted me to omit her name from the Introduction,'
he stated after her death. This was done.

Thus on the feast of St Catherine, 25 November
1535, the Company first took recognizable shape. On
that day twenty-eight of her companions received
Communion together in the church of S. Afra. When
Mass was over Angela inscribed her name in a book,
specially acquired for the purpose, and below, all the
twenty-eight ladies who were with her did the same.
There was no other ceremony; no distinguishing habit
or head-dress was worn. Exactly fourteen months
earlier, on 15 August 1534, St Ignatius and his six companions had attended Mass and received Communion in
the little chapel outside Paris in Montmartre. As at S.
Afra's, there was no ceremony, nor was there any
formal ecclesiastical approval of their Company. The
two saints had been led in the same way to the simple
inauguration of parallel works.

13

The Rule

It was not Angela's intention that the *Rule* which she dictated to Cozzano should be complete. It covered the first stage in the foundation of the Company and roughly corresponded with the agreements undertaken by St Ignatius' companions at Montmartre.

Her first *Rule* consisted of only twelve chapters. It laid down principles rather than regulations and contained no stipulations for central government, or for the continuity of the Company after the foundress's death. The remaining chapters, namely from Chapter XIII to the end, were promulgated many years later.

All the founders of great religious Orders have been reluctant legislators. In their first draft the *Rules* of St Benedict, St Francis and St Angela were no more than the expression of their personal approach to God: their simple statement of ideals in the pursuit of a spiritual life amounts to little more than an inspired exhortation to follow the pattern of chastity, prayer and good work set by Our Lord. It took Ignatius many years to face the reality that all who joined his Company might not be able to manifest so constantly or with the same intensity the love of God that was the inspiration of his own life. In her humility, Angela, like Ignatius, considered it sufficient to lay down the general principles contained in the first twelve sections. Only after her death were further detailed sections added concerning the external government of the Company in order to ensure harmony among its members and to strengthen the interior spirit when the first inspiration began to weaken. The established practice of religious founders, wrote Ignatius, the advice of prudent men and the command of ecclesiastical authority, were his three reasons for writing *Rules*. For Angela all these three reasons were represented by the person of Gabriel Cozzano.

In the first two and a half years after the first foundation Angela guided the development of the Company. The first significant date in the history of the Confraternity, after the meeting at S. Afra's, was 8 August 1536, when the *Rule* was formally approved by Cardinal Cornaro; thereafter, until her death and under her own direction, there were some further additions made to her original idea. Following her death, there were still more rapid developments as the Company spread beyond Brescia to Milan and other Italian cities.

After the first companions had inscribed their names in the register at S. Afra's, their life continued much as it had run before. It is unlikely that they considered themselves in any strict sense members of a religious institution. They had joined together as a band of women to make more effective by direction from above their desire to counter the disruptive pagan forces in their native city. There was no mention in this first period of a General or Assistants. In so far as there was government, it was in the hands of Gabriel Cozzano, the spiritual director of the Company, who himself represented the bishop.

It is Chapter VIII of the *Rule*, entitled Obedience, that reveals the limits of Angela's first conception. After observing that 'Obedience founded in charity is a source of great light in man, rendering all his works good and acceptable', Angela enumerates those to whom obedience is due, feeling her way, as it were, towards a more strict conception of the religious Order into which the Company was soon to develop. It was the bishop, as the successor of the Apostles and Vicar of the Pope, who was the ultimate Governor of the Confraternity, under God. 'Each one of you should first obey the commandments of God. . . . Secondly, obey him who governs Mother Church, because He who is truth has said: "Who hears you, hears me, and who despises you, despises me."' And then, in descending order, obedience is to be given to priests, the spiritual director, to mother and father, to the laws, statutes and civil authorities.

There is little here that is not an elaboration of Christian precepts binding on all, but later, where she speaks of the spiritual director, she can be seen advancing towards the conception of religious life outside the cloister. She wanted each and all of her companions to be completely under ecclesiastical authority and at the same time alert to the individual direction of the Holy Spirit in submission to the director. 'Over and above all this,' she writes in the most significant paragraph, 'be docile to the divine inspirations, which under the judgement and approval of your spiritual father, you may recognize as coming from the Holy Ghost.'

Here in simple outline are the principles without the prescription of religious obedience. The practice of poverty is recommended but not made binding. 'Each member of the Company', says Angela in her Franciscan way, 'should strive to despoil herself of everything and set all her good, her love, her delight, not in robes, nor in food nor in relatives, but in God alone and in his benign and ineffable Providence.' She states explicitly that neither obedience, poverty nor virginity are the subject of vows, but simply of resolutions. Through the practice of these evangelical counsels above all other means, her companions will receive 'an ever-increasing charity' and become the 'sisters of the angels . . . possessors of all good'.

In this first stage of the Company it is the spiritual director who has the complete and unrestricted powers of government. He is the delegate of the Bishop who, having 'too large a diocese to occupy himself directly with the affairs of the Company', entrusts to his substitute, the director, all matters concerning its government, 'conservation and progress'. To him, not to Angela, obedience is due. He can change anything 'at will as he deems expedient and better for the Company'. No meetings can take place without his presence. He examines candidates and approves them. He is the 'Father and Superior' of all members.

It is clear that Angela, in the first draft of her *Rule*, was legislating merely for a Company of ladies whose work would be directed and inspired by her ideals and who, at the same time, with the approval of their director, Gabriel Cozzano, would be free to follow whatever path along which the Holy Spirit should guide them. She herself had found in Cozzano an adviser of wisdom and discernment and she hoped her followers would benefit as much from his direction as she herself had done. She had always recognized the need for authoritative guidance in the spiritual life. From her childhood she had been on her guard against the deceptions of the devil. Doubtless, among her first companions were ladies who believed themselves specially graced by God, for it was an age of false as well as true mystics and it is unlikely that Brescia differed from other Italian cities in its pursuit of the extraordinary in spiritual experiences. Agostino Gallo points out that Angela herself had met many devout ladies who boasted of their visions, who regularly on Wednesdays and on Fridays entered a kind of coma and, for several hours on end, remained immobile, with arms outstretched, usually in public places. 'There were even some who boasted that they carried on their hands and feet the stigmata of Our Lord's Passion, and had done and seen marvellous things.'

Angela was anxious that this spirit of boastfulness should not infect her companions. Although she herself had many authentic mystical experiences, she kept them to herself and to her director. As Agostino Gallo again remarked, she considered false mystics 'in greater danger of perdition than even infidels, for she knew well that they had been led all the way into error by the demon who, as St Paul says in his second Epistle to the

Corinthians, transforms himself into an angel of light.'
Indeed, in the Preamble to the *Rule*, she has much to
say on the snares of the devil, and warns her young
followers that their vocation to an unworldly life does
not in itself protect them from the deceits of Satan.
On the contrary, 'the greater and more valuable the
enterprise, the more fatigue and danger you incur:
there is no way out of evil except by opposing it'.
Pride does not die on signing the register of admission;
the devil is merely alerted by their desire to follow an
unselfish life, and he has 'tricks and cunning beyond
recounting to find out in what way he can devour us'.

It is against the background of religious hysteria and
claims to extraordinary mystical graces that the first
twelve chapters of Angela's *Rule* must be read. From
beginning to end Angela insists on humility and submission, both at meetings of the Company and, at home,
'to father and mother or other superiors' and this submission is to be without any reserve 'unless there be
something commanded contrary to God's honour and
one's own good and salvation'. And for the same reason
Angela strives in these sections to inculcate solid and
unostentatious devotion. All are to attend Mass every
day 'because in the Holy Mass', and not in any extraordinary personal experiences or manifestations, are
found in a unique way all the merits of the Passion of
Our Lord Jesus Christ. After Mass, members of the
Company are not to attract attention to themselves by
prolonging their prayer. 'If you wish to pray,' she says
with hard sense, 'go into your room and there, retired,

pray as much as your spirit and conscience dictates.'

It would seem that during the early years after the foundation of the Company the only regular meetings of all the members occurred on the first Friday of the month. From her days at Desenzano, Angela had fasted and spent long hours in prayer every Friday in commemoration of the Passion of Our Lord, and it was this devotion that she hoped to impress upon her followers by making the first Friday their day of meeting. During the interval between the meetings, her companions were to go about their work independently, making their home their cloister. There appears to have been no record of her own activity at this time. It would seem that she continued her work exactly as before. Although she was over sixty, she maintained her fasts. For her, fasting was 'the principle and means of all our good and spiritual profit'. And her emphasis on this was so constant that it is likely that she had some special revelation which she made known only to Cozzano. Indeed, solely in the matter of fasting did she lay down any detailed regulations. At the same time, however, she is careful not to overtax her companions. She is anxious that they should not be imprudent. Even for the prescribed fasts they must have the advice of the director who can dispense them as he thinks expedient.

In these paragraphs the Franciscan influence on Angela's *Rule* is apparent. From her days at Salo she had rigidly observed all the fasts laid down in the *Rule* of the Tertiaries. Fasting had made her prayer effective. This was her experience, and now in her own *Rule* she insists that the two are not to be separated. Prayer, mental and vocal, in her own phrase, is 'the companion to fasting', and she supports this by quoting the Scriptural text, 'prayer is good with fasting', and also the practice of the prophetess Anna who is to be their model. Similarly vocal prayer, which 'prepares the mind for mental prayer', is exactly the prayer ordered by the Franciscan Rule, with the same alternative prescriptions of *Paters* and *Aves* for those who cannot read. Only in the prayer of her own composition does she depart from the tradition in which she has been brought up. The offering of the faculties of the soul to God, which bears an astonishing likeness to Ignatius Loyola's, is her own. Here is the spirit of St Angela and the ideal she sought to inspire into others. The language of the prayer is in part traditional, in part most individual, particularly in the passage that seems to span her life's experience from Grezze to S. Afra's, in which she asks God 'to forgive the sins of my father and mother, of my relatives and friends, and of all the world. I pray for this by thy most holy Passion, by thy most precious blood shed for love of us and by thy sacred name, Jesus. May it be blessed in heaven and on earth and by all the heavenly choirs of angels and archangels.'

In its framework the first section of the Primitive *Rule* was inspired by the Franciscan *Rule*, not in the direct sense that it was modelled on it, but indirectly, in so far as it expressed Angela's own aspirations and her way of living that had been moulded by it. To Angela herself her *Rule* was 'the *Rule* that God has offered her' and her companions. It was admirably suited to the needs of those who were anxious to model their lives on hers. At the time she composed it she can have had little conception of founding a religious Order: that role was later thrust on her by the expansion of her work in Brescia itself between 1534 and 1537. The link between her own and the later sections of the *Rule* is Chapter XII, which foreshadows the governmental structure of the Company.

14

Development

On 8 August 1536 Lorenzo Mucio, the Vicar-General of Cardinal Cornaro, Bishop of Brescia, gave formal approval to the Primitive *Rule* of St Angela, and in his letter of approbation commended it as 'divine, holy and salutary'.

Among the different dates suggested by biographers of St Angela for the foundation of her Company, the date of the formal ecclesiastical sanction of the *Rule* is both the most common and exact. The enrolment of names in the Book of Companions nine months earlier was a first step towards her foundation, but it gave no official ecclesiastical sanction to her work. It was merely the personal endorsement of a private apostolic enterprise by Gabriel Cozzano, a zealous curial priest.

The last chapter of Angela's Primitive *Rule* shows how the Company set about its work in the days preceding and immediately following the day of foundation. Manifestly the principal purpose of the appointment of officers in the first draft of the *Rule* was to find ladies, inspired by Angela's ideal, who were prepared to continue and extend her charitable work in the city. Nevertheless, the chapter contains a skeleton plan for the future government of the Company.

The *Rule* lays down that there are to be three groups of officials: maidens, matrons and men. As far as can be seen from the text of the *Rule*, the maidens are the spiritual teachers of the novices, the matrons or married ladies are the business women or women of affairs, concerned with the temporal needs of the Company, and the men the counsellors of the matrons in legal and other business. In Angela's phrase, the maidens 'should act as teachers and guides in the interpretation of the rule of the spiritual life', while the matrons were to be 'as mothers full of solicitude for the welfare of their daughters and spiritual sisters. The four men act on behalf of both maidens and matrons as fathers in the current needs of the Company.'

The maidens of the *Rule* are given the task of visiting all their 'sisters' living 'here and there in the town'. They are to do this every fortnight, or more or less often as they find it necessary. If their spiritual children meet with obstruction or trials—and here there is a suppressed hint that much of Angela's own earlier work had met with opposition—they are to comfort and strengthen them. As an example of 'obstruction', as Angela calls it, she instances the case of their 'Superiors'— and here she means their parents or guardians—who do them a wrong or hold them back from some good or even expose them to the occasion of sin. The ensuing quarrel or misunderstanding may involve the family of a companion or be a tangle of worldly as well as purely spiritual considerations, and in these cases, if the maidens find themselves unable to settle it themselves, they 'must refer it to the matrons, and if they cannot settle it, all should meet, including the four men, and work together to reach an understanding'.

REGOLA

Della noua compagnia di santa Orsola
di Brescia : per laquale si vede come
si habbiano a gouernar le vergi‑
ni di detta compagnia accio‑
che viuédo christianamen‑
te possino doppo la
lor morte fruir i
beni di vita
eterna,

In Brescia per Damiano Turlino.

Nel nome della santilsima Triñita, co/
mincia il prologo della vita delle vergi/
ni di nouo principiata col nome della
compagnia di santa Orsola,
τ ad essa dedicato.

Proemio.   Cap. primo.

Di che voi figliole, et
sorelle mie dilettissime
DIo vi ha cócessa gra/
tia, di separarui dalle
tenebre di questo mise/
ro mondo: et vnirue in/
sieme a seruire a sua di/
nina maesta, haueti da renderli in/
finite gratie, che a voi specialmente
habbia concesso cosi singulare do/
no: Impoche quáte persone grandi
saráno, cioe Imperatrici, Regine,
Duchesse, τ simili, che per maggior sua fe
licita, τ lor gloria desideraráno di essere
state vna minima ancilla vostra, conside/
rando la códittione vostra esser stata tan/
to piu degna, τ megliore della sua. Onde
sorelle mie vi essorto, anci vi prego, che es/

A ii

This is Angela, the tireless peacemaker, appearing in her own *Rule* in spite of her effort to conceal herself. At the time of the promulgation of the first *Rule* Angela had done little more than plan an extension of her own work throughout the city. The all-important last chapter of the *Rule* (Chapter XII) incorporates her own experience in directing the apostolate of her friends. In many years of unobtrusive apostolate, she found that she needed the help of well-connected married women; she was aware that there were many problems of peace-making that could not be settled even with their help; and that there were still more complex situations that called for the citizens like Agostino Gallo, who was probably the model of the 'men' who are assigned certain tasks in her *Rule*.

The only definition Angela gives to the position of these 'men' is by way of two hypothetical cases. 'If one of the Sisters,' she writes, 'being an orphan, is kept out of her inheritance, or if a servant . . . cannot, for some reason, obtain her wages, or if anything should occur which obliges her to go to law or to try to come to an agreement (which would be far better), in such a case the four men should act with fatherly kindness and take the matter in hand, helping the Sister according to her need.'

But the men and matrons were not governors; nor were the maidens any more than senior members of the Company elected to initiate the young aspirants in Angela's way of life. The only hint that any governmental responsibility was vested in any members at all, is in a short but vague paragraph which suggests that all three—maidens, matrons and men—acting together have power to keep and spend wisely all money held in common for the Company. The general picture of the organization given by this important last section of the *Rule* is very primitive. Certainly at this stage it cannot be called a religious Order; even the word *Rule* itself is inappropriate, for in its primitive form it is more exactly a charter for charitable activity of a group of devout ladies in the city of Brescia. Its inspiration is Franciscan, and it concludes with instructions for the conduct of sisters at the burial of any member of the Company that in general are little different from the prescriptions of the Third Order.

For more than seven months after Cardinal Cornaro had given his approbation to the Rule, no officials were elected. It was on 18 March 1537 that the first elections were held. Four maidens and four widows were elected. The election of the four men was postponed until later. These officials were, in fact, not appointed either on this occasion or later in Angela's lifetime or after her death.

On the day of election all the members of the Company assembled in the house next to S. Afra's, in the large room adjoining Angela's cell. A detailed account of proceedings is extant in the form of a legal document drawn up by Thadeas de Monte (Thadeas de Montibus), a Brescian lawyer, who was employed by Angela to act as notary. The paper is entitled: *Record of the manner of election of the Mother General, and first of the blessed Mother Angela*. It is preserved in the State Archives of

Brescia.[1] This record of the proceedings is introduced by the names of four witnesses, men from the parish of S. Afra's, and the names are followed by a legal recital of the history of the Company, or, as it is alternatively called, the Confraternity. Here Angela is styled 'the Venerable Sister Angela'—an indication that in her last years she was regarded as a saint by her contemporaries: and she is then legally identified, so to speak, as a member of the Third Order of Franciscan Observantines and as the daughter of Giovanni Merici, late citizen of the province of Brescia (no mention is made of Desenzano). From this it is clear that Angela, even to the end of her life, regarded her Confraternity as a body existing within the framework of the Franciscan *Rule*: and that she never ceased to consider herself, even after the foundation of her Company, a Franciscan Tertiary. Indeed, not only were many of the practical precepts of her *Rule* Franciscan in derivation: but her dress, her fasts and prayers to the end were the same as she had adopted during her childhood at Salo. The reference to the Observantine branch of Franciscans in the deed of foundation would seem a further indication that it was at Salo, where the Observantines served the church, that she joined the Third Order.

The historical recital of the foundation goes on to mention the fact that two years previously the Con-

[1] A full transcript is printed in an appendix to Mother Cecilia Lubienska's book, Ojczyna sw Angeli i Jej Zycie (1935), and is sub-titled *Registro delli Instrumenti per l'ellettioni delle Madre General, et primo della Beata Madre Angela*, pp. 344–7.

fraternity had received the approval and praise of the
Vicar-General of the Cardinal Bishop, namely Laurentio
Mucio, who was also his *locum tenens*. This was on 8
August 1536, when the Vicar had confirmed the Primitive *Rule* of twelve chapters. Particular mention is made
of Chapter XI of the *Rule*,[1] even to the folio number
(folio twenty-two of the original manuscript), which
makes provision for the election of the four maidens,
four matrons and the four men, who, in this place are
described as 'agents and spiritual fathers in the wants
and worries of the Company'.

After this, the document comes to the object of the
meeting, or as it is described later, the Chapter. A head
of the Company is elected. It is difficult to say to what
extent Angela had foreseen the course of events on this
day; or how far she herself influenced the discussions of
the Chapter. In her humility and in keeping with the
spirit of the Third Order of St Francis, she would not
permit herself as head of the Company to be described
as a Superior; this office, she insisted, still belonged to
the curial priest, Gabriel Cozzano. Possibly if Angela
on this occasion had been able to persuade her companions that she was altogether unsuited to become their
head, the constitution of the Company would have
been different: but, as all anticipated, Angela herself
was elected, not as Superior, but simply as the 'mistress,
treasurer or prioress', with a brief, not to govern the
maidens and matrons, but to regulate the alms and

[1] This is now printed as Chapter XII, which begins: 'It has
been decided that for the government . . . '

legacies made over to the Company, and, in particular, to exact the *livella* left to the Company by its first benefactor, Agostino Patengola.

By age alone Angela considered herself disqualified from election. There is no doubt that she wanted to have as the first Mother of the Company a woman in her prime, with some experience both in secular affairs and in the direction of the young. She knew, moreover, that her health was precarious and that she had only a few years to live. There was no question that it was her hope that the first Mother, selected as she was for life, should be a lady still young enough to give promise of a long period of office during which the traditions of the new Company should become firmly established.

It says much for Angela's conception of her own position that in this deed of government, so to call it, her own powers were exclusively temporal. What is unrecorded in the document is perhaps more significant than what is, in fact, stated. Since there is no other authentic account of the discussions that led to her election, it is not fanciful to presume that when her companions showed their unanimous intention to elect her Superior or General of the new-born Company, she refused, and agreed only to govern its temporal affairs, for which her connections in Brescia made her the obvious choice. However, the office that she agreed to accept did, in fact, develop into that of Superior; and in the remaining three years of her life she set the pattern of government which was incorporated into later drafts of the *Rule*. As the recital states, it was necessary both for the preservation and continuance of the Company that someone should be elected to exercise authority over the body; and from this beginning it was natural that her authority should later be extended over the lives of the individuals who made it up.

The acts of the first Chapter at S. Afra's, on 18 March 1537, make it clear that Angela's purpose in convoking it was to gain protection for the Company and guarantee its continuation after her death. This is stated in as many words.

The proccedings began with the invocation of the Blessed Trinity. Then votes were cast. Fifty-nine members of the Company were present, thirteen absent. *Viva voce* and unanimously Angela was elected 'mother, mistress and treasurer' for life; and at the same time it was decreed that after Angela's death one of the maidens more advanced in years, whose qualifications for government had been tested, was to preside over the Company in her place. This done, the Chapter proceeded to elect the four maidens and the matrons. Their names were listed, and to the four matrons a fifth was added. Such executive authority that the body was given rested with them: and it was accepted that all they did or decided should be as binding as if done or decided by the whole Company. However, if one or other of these officials died or for some reason was unable to continue in office, then her successor was to be selected in Chapter either by the whole Company or a majority of its members.

The proceedings of the Chapter established the general lines along which the Company was to develop. The complete list of those present, which follows the record of proceedings, shows how even at this early stage in its history Angela's Company had already extended beyond Brescia: there were companions present from many of the cities and towns of the Lombard plain, from Verona, Cremona, Monticelli, Leno, Bovengo, Martinengo and other places. Strangely there were none from the towns of Lake Garda. Here and there a description is added to a name by way of identification and, at the end of the list, occurs that of 'Flora, the servant of Jerome Patengola', Angela's first friend in Brescia. The fifty-nine present were from all classes of society, and formed a group similar in social composition to the Tertiaries of St Francis.

During the last three years of her life Angela, with great diplomacy, appears for the most part to have left the direction of the Company in the hands of others, taking care that it should be governed on a plan that would be unaffected by her own death. Already she foresaw its rapid development and at the same time was anxious not to make the framework of the Company so rigid that it would be unable to adapt itself to the needs of the struggling Church in north Italy, which, in her modest conception, it was designed to assist.

15

Last Years

Before the almost total destruction of S. Afra's church in March 1945, there hung on the walls a framed painting showing Angela seated in the centre of six of her early companions. Five were the matrons of the Company, whose names are mentioned in the recital of the acts of the first Chapter. Elizabeth Prato is on Angela's left, the Countess Luzzago and Donna Maria Avogadro on her right: the remainder are not identified.

The painting summarizes the last years of Angela's apostolate in Brescia, years devoted to the training of the officials of her Company in the spirit of the *Rule*. Her role was now that of teacher and mistress. Thus she sits raised on a dais above her companions. She appears unusually tall for a woman known to have been below average height; the athletic childhood frame is now drawn and worn, her expression gentle and almost smiling. The six companions wear a simple bonnet of linen contrasting with Angela's white veil that hangs down over her shoulders. Her left hand holds an open book on her knee, her right is lifted with the fingers outstretched to emphasize a point in the instructions she is giving her matrons.

If the traditional dating of the picture is correct, it was done soon after her death and is the oldest of the authentic portraits of Angela: and for this reason has great interest. In sharper prints of the original it is still possible to see the same features that are portrayed in other paintings of St Angela lost when S. Afra's was destroyed—her angular nose, slightly rounded at the end, the raised nostrils, her broad and gently arched mouth and long protruding chin. Although the painting was not the work of a great artist, it conveyed the authority exercised by Angela in the three short years she lived after her election as Mistress.

This is an unchronicled period, but the most important in her life. The single recorded fact is that she continued to live at S. Afra's: there is no mention of any pilgrimage beyond Brescia, or indeed of any work done within the city, apart from the training of her disciples in the spirit of obedience and motherly care which was her legacy to them. The vision of Brudazzo was now fulfilled: and it was her last task to remain faithful to its message and to transmit it unimpaired to her companions. The apparent restlessness of her middle years was only a desperate search for a clarification of her task. Now that the task was clear, her failing effort was concentrated on its completion.

In all but the more recent books on St Angela the Primitive *Rule* is laid out in twenty-four chapters, without any distinction between the first part, which was written at her dictation, and the last twelve sections, which were added some thirty-seven years after her death without any revision of the first part. There are obvious inconsistencies between the two sections, most noticeably in the matter of government, for while the Governor of the Company in the first section is the

Spiritual Father, in the second it is the Mother General. Nevertheless it is apparent that the last chapters faithfully incorporate the customs of the Company and Angela's own manner of governing it during her years as Mistress. It is likely also that certain phrases in the second part are hers, orally passed down by those who at the time were still young enough to remember her teaching with verbal exactness; and it contains other passages also that are derived from her *Counsels*. For this reason it cannot be considered merely the embodiment of a later development after her death. There is no conflict between these later Constitutions and Angela's established teaching. It is even possible that the final version of these last twelve chapters, written in Milan in the year 1581, is based on a much earlier document which summarized Angela's own oral instructions to her companions at their fortnightly meetings. This would also explain how the whole body of the Constitutions was without question accepted as Angela's own Primitive *Rule*. It is known that Angela herself impressed on her companions the need for developing the regulations concerning government that she herself laid down. While she acted as Mistress of the Company, she was without question accepted in fact as its Superior, although she herself never allowed it to be acknowledged that she was more than its Administrator. But in her *Testament* and *Counsels* she shows herself aware that her successor would be forced to accept the position of Superior that she herself declined. And it is unlikely in any case that these later chapters would have been

accepted by her early companions unless they had faithfully registered Angela's own practice and her precise
directions.

During these last years Angela, through Gabriel
Cozzano, petitioned Pope Paul III for approval of her
Confraternity by the Holy See. Angela would certainly
have discussed this step with her Council, for it implied
the addition of more detailed governmental regulations
to the *Rule*. It was easy to see how the simple framework
of the *Rule* approved by Cardinal Cornaro could be
expanded into a rather more elaborate structure for
submission to the Pope. Only in this way could her
Congregation, which was still diocesan, become not
only national in character, but even world-wide.

Indeed, in these last years Angela reached the full
understanding of her vision at Brudazzo, and was given
the grace to see how the Company which was now
formed was to endure and expand. It was more than
likely that the petition framed by Cozzano at Angela's
prompting outlined the detailed developments which
were later incorporated in the last twelve chapters of the
Rule. There is little doubt also that many of the stipulations of this section were already in force in Angela's
time. 'The petition [to Pope Paul III]', writes Gabriel
Cozzano, 'was written by my hand, but its contents
came from the Holy Spirit through the Foundress.'

At the same time Cozzano's influence on the shape of
the Primitive *Rule* is apparent. It is possible that at Rome
he had experience in framing Constitutions for the new
religious orders that were now forming to combat the

influence of heresy. Certainly Cardinal Cornaro, in whose name the *Rule* was approved, during his long years at the Papal Court had taken part in discussions on the *Rule* of the new Societies founded by Jerome Aemiliani and John Cajetan. As has been seen, it was not an uncommon experience of Roman officials to introduce to the reigning Pope a zealous priest or devout woman who was anxious to submit for oral approval not so much the Rule of a new religious order, as an outline of common life. Many such schemes were still-born; others flourished and grew into the new religious Congregations. From her travels in the cities of northern Italy, Angela was familiar with many of them. Their Constitutions provided a rough pattern for hers; for like her own Company these societies had their origin locally in the initiative of a single person. Starting as regional bodies, they later became national, like her own, and finally universal. Cozzano, with Cardinal Cornaro at hand for consultation, appears to have been admirably equipped to draft by his 'hand' the governmental structure of St Angela's Company, which she herself was incapable of working out in detail.

It was axiomatic that approval by the Holy See of a Society that was to extend beyond the boundaries of a single diocese carried with it the appointment of a Mother General, for such sanction made it no longer practicable for a local diocesan official, such as Gabriel Cozzano, to govern a Confraternity that Papal appro-bation had made universal in the Church. In her humility Angela never accepted the name either of

Foundress or General, although in the acts of the first Chapter she allowed herself to be called *auctrix* or initiator. Knowing now that she had only a few years of life, she set about the further development of the Constitutions, and it was for this reason, as well as for her obvious suitability for the post, that she had consented to the unanimous vote of the companions that she should act as head of the Company. Her own practice as Mistress would seem to have inspired these later chapters of the Primitive *Rule*.

Gradually, during this last period, Gabriel Cozzano, as Superior still of the Company, yielded place to Angela, but remained constantly at her side always, more in the capacity of spiritual adviser than Governor. The Company was growing more quickly than even the first Chapter had anticipated. Its members were now being drawn from other towns besides Brescia, and the position of the Mistress inevitably developed into that of Superior.

'Let there be a Mother General of the Company whose office shall be for life and who shall be elected by a two-thirds majority of those who take a part in the election.' This opening phrase of the second part of the *Rule* reflects exactly the first intentions of the Chapter that elected Angela. Unity of government was her aim; it was endorsed by her companions and later plainly asserted in the *Rule*. There must be 'one Superior over the whole Company, so that not many but one may do the ruling'. This without question is Angela's mind, and the mind also of Cozzano, and is reflected time and

again, as will be seen, in her *Testament* and *Counsels*.
Angela found many ways of reiterating the importance
she attached to a single and central government. While
she foresaw, countenanced and provided in her *Counsels*
for change, it was to be change always within one
governmental system. Splintering and division she
regarded as characteristics of heresy. The Company in
its infancy was under the local ecclesiastical authority:
before her death she had already taken steps to see that
its government under a Superior should depend
directly upon the Holy See. In no other way could it
expand and become an instrument of the Church in
other cities in the struggle against the Reformers.

The interest of the sections dealing with the Mother
General of the Company rests in this: that it is an exact
portrait from the recollections of the first companions
of the way in which Angela governed the Company in
the years between her election and her death. The
pattern of her own behaviour was the inspiration of this
section of the *Rule*. Like St Ignatius and in almost the
same phrasing, Angela demands as the first qualification
of the Superior 'extraordinary union with God', so that
the Holy Spirit, who is truly to direct the Company,
should find in her an apt instrument. St Ignatius himself, in his sketch of the General of the Order, further
required of him a blameless life and the example of
virtue, combined with strength to bear the weaknesses
of his subjects, to face opposition and to undertake great
enterprises. Only after these qualities were intelligence
and experience mentioned. Similarly, though with less

precision of language, the same qualities are to be sought in the Superior of Angela's Company: her own virtue is to give her authority and her example should encourage all to aspire to perfection; 'she should be mature in mind rather than advanced in years' and known as a person of great charity so that with true maternal feeling she may be quick to help all members of the Company in need of her comfort.

It is significant that in her *Rule* and still more in her *Counsels* Angela strives to get as far away as possible from the type of Superior she had known in her childhood—the great dame of the cloister who was no true mother of the community. She never ceased to impress on her companions the need of gentleness in dealing with young ladies, particularly those in distress. If other qualifications were equal, Angela was anxious that a maiden rather than a matron should be Superior, for an unmarried woman 'would resemble more those whom she was set to govern', and thus the young members of the Company would, in the quaint phrasing of the *Rule*, be more confident of finding 'great love and charity in one who had been its own daughter, nourished, so to speak, with its own milk'.

The remaining sections of the second part of the Primitive *Rule*, besides registering the practice of Angela in these years, indicate the end towards which she was striving. Angela's own health was failing. There were times when she was compelled to hand over the direction of the Company to a Vicar. And in the *Rule* the Vicar, who is to stand for the Superior in her absences or sickness, is appointed by the Assistants of the Superior. (Already the four maidens and five matrons are becoming Assistants.) She is to take charge of the Company, as Donna Lucrezia did, on the death of the Superior until a successor is appointed. Every week (and here the practice of Angela's last year of office is formalized) the Assistants are to meet in Council under the presidency of the Superior in order 'to discuss current matters, to provide for the needs of the Company and to treat of business'.

The great interest for an historian of these sections is that they reproduce exactly what is known of the practice of St Ignatius at Rome during the years when these Constitutions of Angela's Company were still being written. It is impossible to say from what source the influence came: but the similarity of practice is striking: and it may indeed be traceable to a friend of Cardinal Cornaro or Gabriel Cozzano in the Roman Court, whose task and genius it was to establish a system of government that was designed for the urgent problems of the new Orders.

In Angela's own lifetime the structure of the Company was already becoming hierarchical. This was inevitable and the common development of all Congregations founded under the pressure of heresy. Nevertheless Angela's spirit breathes through the last sections of the *Rule* as it does in the first. Throughout it is Angela who is speaking phrases that combine spiritual insight with constitutional precepts. Thus, for example, the *Rule*, in its summary of the way Governors should behave towards their subjects, urges them, in the authentic language of its Foundress, to 'love with a fine and deep love the sisters under their protection'; and, in a passage that could have been written only by a woman, tells them that it is their duty to behave 'with such love as they owe to the very dear spouses and beloved children of Jesus Christ, striving to enfold them in a maternal tenderness; not looking on them as mean and ordinary women, but loving and recognizing in them the God for whose love they have undertaken their charge'. At the same time Angela stressed the duty of affection and obedience in the members of the Company equally with the obligation of charity in the Superior. The Superior was to behave as Christ, while the subject was to obey Christ in the Superior.

As Angela first conceived it, the Company was founded and organized for charitable works in Brescia, and indeed the number of officials was dictated by the number of *podestas* or municipal divisions of the city; but during her brief rule as Mistress of the Company the expansion was so rapid that she could legislate only by custom, example and precept. The pattern she set was to inspire with her spirit and method those with whom the succession and development lay.

16

Death

Towards the end of December 1539 Angela became ill. Since the early autumn she had been failing in health, but she continued to direct the Company, though towards the end she delegated more of her tasks to the Contessa Lucretia di Lodrone. Her interest now was more in the spiritual instruction of her daughters than in the direction of their work. Her thoughts were on the phrasing and content of the last Testament she was to leave to them.

Nevertheless, whenever she had the strength, she continued to see visitors, either aspirants to the Company, or, as in her first days in Brescia, men and women in spiritual or temporal distress. Now, as six years earlier when she was thought to be dying in the house that Agostino Gallo had rented in Cremona, many of her callers came from curiosity, to see the lady who was already declared blessed by the citizens, to receive a word of counsel or simply to glance at her at prayer. Many callers were the parents or brothers and sisters of her companions. From the very scarce records of these last weeks, it is clear that she retained to the end her appreciation of persons and occasions. When Giacomo Chizzola entered her room she raised herself on her couch and gave him a long discourse on the true Christian life. With Thomaso Gavardo she was brief. Thomaso begged her to let him take away some 'spiritual testament', but she only answered: 'Do in life what you would wish to have done at the hour of death.'

What Angela herself called her last *Testament* was, in fact, read to her Company by Gabriel Cozzano a month after her death. It summarized her instructions during the months of her last illness. Virginity and motherhood are the two ideas that were central to her thought at this time; and it was through the realization of this twofold vocation that she aimed at the reform of Brescian society. She feared that as the Company grew, its government might become less personal. 'I beseech you, bear each one of your sisters individually in your hearts,' she exhorted them, 'and not merely their names, but the conditions in which they live, their character and disposition—in short, their whole lives', and she urged them to 'love all their daughters with equal affection, so that they might have no more pronounced fondness for one than for the rest'. 'Remember,' she added, 'it is always right to love one's mother whether she be good or faulty.'

Here, in her last instructions, Angela revealed the secret of her own influence during her twenty-five years in Brescia; for all who had come to her for help found no common or ready-made remedy, but a concern for their own individual problems. And there is a passage in her *Counsels* which is her last known prayer and recalls her early struggles in Brescia as a peacemaker among warring families and alliances. 'I address to you as a prayer my last words which, I repeat, I would gladly write with my blood—preserve unity and harmony, so that you may have but one heart and one will.'

There are echoes of the psalms in these paragraphs of her *Testament*, phrases which had become part of her life through her daily recitation of the office, and echoes also of the letters of St Paul. 'Act, bestir yourselves, have confidence, strive, cry to Him from the bottom of your heart, and without doubt you will see wonders.'

Here in her *Testament* and in her *Counsels* is the spirit of the Primitive *Rule* and the spirit of the Order to which it was to give rise. At one time Angela is setting out the highest ideal of obedience, at another stressing the importance of courtesy and good manners. Discretion and breeding must always appear in the speech of her companions and their dealings with others: familiarity of any kind must be avoided, even with their own spiritual fathers, 'for too great spiritual familiarity nearly always degenerates into carnal familiarity'. As throughout her life, now, so to speak, with her last physical effort, she exhorts her children to beware of any taint of unorthodoxy. They need to be cautious always even in their choice of directors and must 'take care that no confessor or religious turns a maiden away from any of her good resolutions, whether it be fasting or a firm determination to observe virginity or the esteem of their divinely ordained *Rule*'. Such conduct would cause the break-up of the Company and the destruction of all that Angela had sought to achieve. 'Frequent reception of the Sacraments, particularly Penance and the Holy Eucharist', with fasting and virginity, are to be the foundations of their spiritual life. Like St Ignatius, Angela was aware from experience that there was no danger of self-deception here. It is as though in her last months she had foreseen with great clarity that her Company would become an instrument against heresy. At no price would she admit novelties in teaching that might endanger the doctrinal foundation of the virginity she sought from her followers. St Ursula was her patron: the primitive esteem for the consecrated life in women, which she had learnt at the tombs of the early Brescian martyrs, was to inspire the new followers of the virgin martyr. Paul III had not yet confirmed her *Rule*: this delay may well have made her reflect that changes were to come: and this was the time to make it clear in what matters she would counsel no alteration whatsoever.

Nowhere else and at no other time was Angela so forthright in speaking of herself. Only as she approached her end did she accept the acknowledgement of the Company that she was its Mother and Foundress. Possibly she foresaw the difficulties and differences that were to arise later, for, in several places, in her brief last *Souvenir*, she stresses that her work of guidance and protection will continue after her death. Then she will be 'more truly alive' than when she was in this world: she will 'see better and care more greatly for the good works' of the Company, will help them more effectively and 'do them good in every way'. And in almost the last passage she urges Gabriel Cozzano to tell her companions that then she will be yet 'more alive than when they saw me in the flesh': that she will be able to 'see and know better and will help them more'; that she will be 'constantly in their midst with Him who is my Love (or rather ours), provided they have faith and never lose courage or hope.' Thus will they grow in strength and expand in numbers.

Angela had no fear of death: indeed, she showed some impatience in the act of dying. At Montebello and on her voyage back from Crete to Venice her physical bravery had inspired courage in her fellow pilgrims. Now this quality did not desert her, and it was joined with an exquisite courtesy.

Her fever was of a lingering character. Early in January 1540 she knew she was dying. Her last exhortation was full of concern for others. In one brief passage in particular she summarized the secret of her influence. 'Beware,' she warned her companions, 'that you do not try to accomplish anything by force, for God has given every single person free will and He desires to constrain none. He merely shows them the way, invites and counsels them; as in the words of St John, "I counsel you to buy an incorruptible crown." "I counsel you," he says, not "I force you." '

Her conception of the calling of her companions, although it was later made the subject of much controversy, was without question an extension of her own life of peacemaking and instruction. Her insistence in the last days of her life on the nobility of this calling is a reflection of her state of intense happiness, and it was this happiness that she longed to give as her last bequest to all the members of the Company. 'There is none that surpasses it'—'Greet my companions,' she tells Gabriel Cozzano. 'Exhort them to persevere in the life they have begun, urge them to long for the blessed and eternal triumph': and, with this in the forefront of the mind, they must feel 'no regret for the heavy charge that is laid on them': for theirs is a vocation, as she had constantly insisted, that surpasses in splendour the status of an exalted princess or great lady of the court.

This was Angela's conversation during the last months of her life. Her constant visitor was Gabriel Cozzano, who was the second founder of the Company. To him she dictated these precepts that she entitled her *Testament*. Since they were to be read to her companions only after her death, she was able to speak with an authority which she had never asserted in her life and to speak about herself in phrases that did not endanger her humility. In her lifetime she proclaimed to no one the confidence she had in her vision at Brudazzo. Only Cozzano knew her secret: had he been permitted to tell it, the task of her biographers would have been easier and the history of the Company different. He was silent. A few short statements of his survive in which he transfers to Angela any credit he himself was given for the conception or organization of the Company.

Angela died on 27 January. On the Sunday before her death a cousin of hers from Salo had come to attend Sung Mass in the Cathedral of Brescia. In the course of his sermon the celebrant had asked prayers for Sister Angela, who lay dying. The young man, Angela's cousin, a Biancosi, probably the son of Bartolomeo Biancosi who had accompanied Angela to the Holy Land, went straight to Angela's room in S. Afra's. Angela stood washing her hair. They talked cheerfully together, Angela recalling perhaps her own girlhood days there under the tutelage of the young man's parents. The youth left comforted by what he saw: it appeared that Angela was far from death. But earlier the same Sunday she had sent her own nurses to church; and while they were absent, she had washed and dressed herself unassisted: she had intended to save them that task after she was dead. Then she asked to be given the Last Sacraments; and after the priest had come, she again called her companions who were in attendance, and took her leave of them, with a last exhortation to persevere in their calling.

Each one of her last actions was a considered completion of her career. She had put on the habit of the Third Order of St Francis, tying her girdle, from which hung her rosary, about her waist and wrapping her white veil over her head. As she had lived, so she would die: a Tertiary, in the habit that was given to her as a girl at Salo. At her request attendants laid her on the mat on which she had slept during her years at S. Afra's, her head resting on a wooden pillow. At that moment she seemed to pass into an ecstasy. Her open eyes were cast upward in a fixed gaze. Several of her companions gathered around her and remarked on the extraordinary brilliance in her eyes which betrayed none of the dullness of approaching death. She held a crucifix in her hands. From time to time she said softly the words, 'Jesus, Jesus.' Then, at the end of their vigil they saw her suddenly awake from her ecstasy, as though she was determined to appear like the rest of the world in the last act of her life. With her native courtesy, perfected by her long intimacy with the saints, she turned her gaze on her nurses, to thank them for their care, and then, without any speech, looked towards her confessor, who was reciting the prayers for the dying. It was her last act of gratitude. Such words she had strength to utter were reserved for God: she spoke them in a clear and gentle voice, in Latin. *In manus tuas, Domine, commendo spiritum meum.* Then she died.

It was exactly half past nine on the evening of Tuesday, 27 January 1540. Two days later her body was carried into the church of S. Afra. During the previous night the whole city had learned of her death.

As her body, placed on a tall bier, rested in the nave of the church, an unceasing procession of citizens filed past. It was a scene similar to that painted by Carpaccio in the Scuola S. Ursula in Venice. For thirty days she lay unburied, her face uncovered. In that interval many churches fought for the honour of receiving her body. The Canons of S. Afra claimed that she was attached to their Oratory and should be buried there; the Franciscans, at the other end of the city, showed that it was in the *Rule* of Tertiaries that she must be buried in their

church with other members of the Order; the priests
of the Cathedral also made out their case. It was the
kind of dispute that Angela had so often witnessed over
the possession of relics of the saints.

However, before her death she herself had taken
steps to settle the question. In 1526, after her visit to
Pope Clement VII, she had sought an Indult giving her
exemption from the *Rule* of the Tertiaries that prescribed burial in their own ground. She had been
granted her request and given liberty to arrange for her
body to be interred in S. Afra's or wherever she decided
according to her devotion. The text of the Papal letter
is extant, dated 4 November 1531 and signed by Filippe
Ferrini, Prefect of the Sacred Penitentiary, on the oral
instruction of the Pope himself.

Thus the remains of Angela of Salo, as she was
described in the Indult, were placed beside the bones of
the martyrs of Brescia in S. Afra's. During the thirty
days that her body lay on a bier in the crypt it was
clothed in the habit of a Tertiary of St Francis. It showed
no signs of death: every joint was flexible as in life and
the skin fresh.

From the accounts of her lying-in-state, Angela's
bier must have resembled the bier of St Ursula in the
famous series of paintings by Carpaccio. Certainly the
similarity of the two scenes inspired Angela's friend,
the Brescian artist Moretto, to attempt a like composition. Until the destruction of S. Afra's this painting
of his hung in the church with another smaller portrait
done by the same artist at the same time. Later this

small picture was copied many times: it is without question the most authentic portrayal of her features, but it lacks the alertness that impressed itself so vividly on her contemporaries.

During her lifetime Angela had been successful in concealing from her friends all uncommon graces that had been given to her in prayer. But during the first three nights that her body lay in the crypt there were many witnesses to an extraordinary and inexplicable phenomenon in the night sky. Over the roof of the church, suspended above the spot where her body lay, a star of great splendour was seen. The Canons of S. Afra's testified to this as well as many citizens, who gave sworn statements of their observations. It was said to be so bright that it attracted to Brescia and to S. Afra's many people from outlying places.

On the thirtieth day, when all the citizens had paid honour to her remains, the burial service was carried out. Her body was dressed in the clothes which it wears today. The Franciscan habit is grey, almost buff now with age. A white girdle is tied round her waist, a lily, the symbol of virginity, rests in her left hand, the staff of a pilgrim in her right. Her head, leaning to one side, lies on a white pillow frilled with gilt lace-work. A pleated bib of linen surrounds her delicate neck. She wears black slippers over white socks and a copy of the *Rule* rests beside her.

The body was placed in a fine tomb provided by the Canons of S. Afra in the section of the crypt below the high altar, close to the sarcophagus containing the bones of the early martyrs of Brescia.[1] The inscription on her first tomb is now let into the wall of the crypt, alongside some fragmentary Christian inscriptions of the third and fourth centuries. It ends: *Quid nisi terram terra regit. Spiritus astra tenet.*

The earth could claim only her bones; her soul had reached the end of its pilgrimage, not the Jerusalem seen from Mount Sion, nor Caimi's at Varallo, but the heavenly Jerusalem of her vision at Brudazzo.

[1] The sarcophagus is now empty. The bones it contained have since been transferred to a reliquary below the high altar in the church.

17

The Company

A month after Angela's funeral the Contessa Lodrone invited all the members of the Company to a Chapter. More than one hundred and fifty assembled for it at the oratory in the cathedral square. The first act of those present was to express their loyalty to their new Superior. A letter from Cardinal Cornaro was then read confirming the Contessa in her office.

The new Superior recalled how Angela, when she was near to death, had given her companions her last *Counsels*. Now she laid before them another document. Angela had entitled it her *Testament* and had dictated it to Gabriel Cozzano who was then asked to read it to the Chapter. It was addressed to 'The Contessa Lucrezia, the principal Mother of the Company of St Ursula, and to the other Governors and Mothers'. There followed a list of matrons and maidens which was itself a summary of Angela's life-work, for it contained the names of families that had been long at war with one another before Angela's first arrival in Brescia, and of others drawn from every level of Brescian society. Here, at this first meeting after Angela's death, they were united in a peace which was largely of her bringing, bound by their vocation to an apostolate that was to assure Brescia for many centuries a vigorous Catholic life. In fact, only when her dead body lay in the crypt of S. Afra's did her example have its full impact, both in the city of her adoption and throughout the northern plain of her native Italy.

Angela's *Testament*, like her *Rule*, is Franciscan both in shape and spirit. On first reading, the most unexpected passage in it is the conclusion: 'Hold it for certain truth', says Angela, 'that this *Rule* of conduct was fashioned by God's holy hand'; then follows the prophecy that 'God never will abandon the Company as long as the world will last. Do not doubt it. I know what I am saying.'

It is as though Angela, after taking care that her statement should be read only after her death, no longer feared to refer to her visions or the special enlightenment given to her by God. Such an emphatic assertion, while she yet lived, would have been out of keeping with her self-abasement before God. Now she was no longer with her companions, a partial revelation of the special favours she had received was needed to encourage them to persevere. And she made it emphatically.

Like the *Testament* of St Francis and the last Epistle of St John, Angela's *Testament* is an exhortation to the love of God. All three saints had lived through times of destruction and had witnessed hatred among nations. Factions at home and strife abroad in the fifteenth as much as in the twelfth century divided Christians confronted with a common enemy. Angela's Company, like the Order of St Francis, could bring peace to people only if it had in itself the spirit of love. All her last recorded messages bear on this single theme. Superiors are to be mothers before all else; they are to entice and lead with a kindly hand, having regard for the free will given to each of their subjects; they are to counsel rather than compel. 'Even if mothers according to nature', Angela writes, 'had a thousand children, they could find room for them all in their hearts.' The expansion of the Company was no excuse for the loss of the spirit that animated its beginnings. Since 'it would seem that the more the number of children grows, the more the mother's love and care increases also', so the Superiors of the Company can and should behave in the same way, 'since spiritual love is beyond comparison more powerful than human love'. This is the love that is to bind them to one another, in heart and will, like 'the Apostles and other Christians of the primitive Church, who had but one heart and one soul'.

It might be St Francis speaking. Unlike St Francis, however, Angela, with the practical sense of a child of Lake Garda, legislates for the possession of property and gives counsel on its administration. While Angela always exhorted followers to almsgiving which, as she learnt from her own practice, 'can withdraw creatures from the path of evil and lead them to good', she foresees that her Company cannot survive, still less increase, unless it is able to possess goods as a corporation. 'If it had not been useful and fitting', she argues, 'for the Company to own property, God would not have thus provided from the beginning': but whatever money it possesses must be used with discretion for the extension of its work.

Since Angela, at least at the time of the foundation of the Company, did not think of it as a religious Order, with vows of obedience and poverty, this question of corporate possession was not perhaps so acute a problem for her as it was for St Francis, whose spirit formed her companions, or for St Ignatius, whose new Order, destined to work alongside her own, received official approval in the year of her death. Angela's approach was direct and practical and not influenced by the study of the Constitutions of other Orders or by the subsequent papal legislation that had modified them. For her the possession of goods, whether in the form of money or property, gave her companions the independence they required for their apostolic activity. During the greater part of her own life in Brescia Angela had been handicapped by her reliance on the hospitality of rich citizens, and only in the few years of her residence at S. Afra did she enjoy the complete freedom she needed for her apostolate. She was determined that her daughters should from the beginning have this benefit which she herself had only towards the close of her life. If they possessed her spirit, they had no cause for worry: almsgiving, charity and fasting were to characterize them, as Cozzano realized so well when he composed the prayer that concluded the ceremony of admission: *Ieunia epulis carnalibus preferant, lectiones sacras et orationes conviviis et potationibus anteparant:* let them value fasting more than feasting, prayer and holy reading more than festive drinking.[1]

[1] First Book of Rules (*Ordine et Ceremonie*), p. 44 (Brescia, 1545).

Angela's greatness as the initiator of a family of religious—she referred to herself, as has been seen, not as foundress but as *auctrix*—is beyond question. She did not map out in detail the lines along which her Company was to develop, but this perhaps was part of her intention. She left her daughters prepared for development along whatever lines the needs of the Church might require. At the time of her death the Council that was to meet at Trent, a day's journey through the hills at the head of Lake Garda, had been summoned, but had not yet assembled. From her conversations with Gabriel Cozzano, and possibly also with Cardinal Cornaro, she had learnt that it was wiser to establish a body of women bound at the start only in a loose association so that later it might be able to adapt itself to the expressed aims of the Council. Until then its members would remain in the lay state, live in their own homes, attend Mass in their parish churches and meet together twice a month for spiritual reading and conferences. The other regulations that she laid down concerned the personal sanctification of its members. They were to lead a retired, unostentatious, mortified life under obedience to their parents and their Superiors in the Company, devoted to good works. No further definition was made, but Angela's example of enterprising charity was taken as a charter. It was natural that her own care for the Christian upbringing of the young unmarried girls of Brescia should later grow into a system of Christian schooling throughout northern Italy and France.

In spite of its loosely conceived structure, Angela's Company was the only organized response among women to the Church's needs in her period. It is also true to say that she was the first woman foundress in her own right. St Scholastica and St Clare had initiated for women counterparts to the Benedictine and Franciscan male families. Angela's Company owed nothing to any pattern of a monastic community. She deliberately rejected the vows of the enclosed Orders and was concerned with a Company that at a time of urgency would restore the primitive spirit of Christianity by reforming the milieu from which its members were drawn. Because their home was to be their cloister, Angela placed her main emphasis on motherly love. Her approach to reform was her own. It was to begin with the family, and from the family to extend to the whole Christian society. The comparative obscurity of her work in a small, though important, city of northern Italy, the lack of adequate documentation (there is not a single letter of hers that has been discovered) and her apparent hesitancy in setting about her life's work, conceal in some measure her true greatness from her biographers.[1] But her stature as a foundress cannot be questioned. In the slow, patient way she set about her task she showed the astonishing courage of a country lady joined to a logic of purpose uncommon in women. From the story of her life emerge the sources of her

[1] A century later Mary Ward was considered a dangerous originator when she attempted the foundation of an Order of women without enclosure. Her aim was identical with Angela's.

inspiration, particularly her single-minded devotion to the early Christian martyrs who took her nearer to Christ in time than the saints of the Middle Ages. She had observed that every reform had professed to be a return to a primitive Christian life: and in the Church as an all-embracing body this was represented by the martyrs. St Paula, whose first tomb she had visited in the cave at Bethlehem, and St Catherine had been inspired by the same desire, and became self-chosen patrons, after St Ursula, of her Company. Even the carefully considered choice of her own burial-place was intended to remind her followers of this inspiration. While she could not foresee the future of her Company, she left in it no uncertainty about the spirit that was to govern it. Had she been more precise in legislating for the shape of her Order, it might well have become hardened too early and lost the vigour and adaptability essential for growth.

The papal confirmation given to her Company four years after her death provided precisely for this growth. While Angela had urged her companions to undertake the Christian instruction of young girls, she had not foreseen that they would become responsible also for their secular education,[1] From the foundation of schools it was only a step towards enclosure in an age that was still unprepared for the idea of a Company of women, pledged to virginity and engaged as free-lance charitable workers under the direction of ecclesiastical

[1] The first school for girls was founded by her Company at Parma in 1595.

authority. Nevertheless, it can be said that the diversity
of work later, and still, undertaken by all the enclosed
nuns, who rightly looked to her as Foundress, was as
great as she conceived for her own first uncloistered
companions: unexpectedly enclosure gave them oppor-
tunities to engage in missionary work at a time when
the Church urgently needed their assistance. Her spirit
of enterprise and her own loyalty to the Papacy would
have without question commended this apostolate to
her, if it had only been considered open to women in
her age. By an accident of history, she also became the
first woman Foundress of an educational Order for
girls that expanded through France and Italy as the
counterpart to the Society of Jesus.

In summary, the story of her life gave little indication
of such a development. There can be no doubt that her
own thinking on the problems of the Church, which is
revealed more in her actions than in any document, set
her apart from her contemporaries, even if her external
life did not make her one of the most remarkable
women of the early Counter-Reformation. There was
little in her upbringing to suggest that she was to play
such an important role in the Church: only in her later
years did she show her qualities of leadership. She
taught no system of prayer, no doctrine that was un-
familiar even in its form; her behaviour, except to those
who observed her closely, was normal. She never came
face to face with the Inquisition, although, as has been
suggested, the late foundation of her Company might
be explained by suspicion of her orthodoxy on the part

of Bishop Paolo Zane, predecessor of Cardinal Cornaro, Bishop of Brescia. While details of her work are rare, her character can be seen with clarity of outline—the strong country-woman, loyal, humble, clinging firmly to the family of saints and the glorious origins of a Church in peril. The mystery of her story lies in the urgency of her mission and her apparent tardiness in fulfilling it. But she was inspired by a new idea, and, historical accidents apart, its immature expression might have meant its ruin. Moreover, as a woman of great saintliness, she was confronted with the perennial problem of initiators of the new families in the Church: the balance between activity and prayer.

There is a harmony in her life and a synthesis. The young child of Grezze, the courageous, independent young girl of Salo became the tireless young traveller of Garda and grew naturally into the great saint of Brescia. The experiences and especially the hardships of her early life moulded her into a foundress. Today her attraction remains unimpaired: the attraction of the pervading simplicity of a saint joined with the shrewd-ness and natural charm of a lady of her countryside of Garda.

Bibliographical Note

Apart from the lives of St Angela listed in Mother M. Monica's *Angela Merici and her teaching ideal* (1927) and other books mentioned in the footnotes, I have drawn also on the following works. They are given here, not as a display of erudition, but as an indication of sources for material not found in other lives of the saint. The place of publication is London unless otherwise stated.

BUTLER, SAMUEL, *Ex Voto, An Account of the Sacro Monte or New Jerusalem at Varallo Sesia*, 1909.

CARTWRIGHT, JULIA, 'Varallo and her painter'. In *The Portfolio, An Artistic Periodical*, 1880, Vol. XI, pp. 50–56.

CAVALCABO, AGOSTINO, *Le Vicende dei nomi delle Contrade di Cremona*. Cremona, 1933.

COLLISON-MORLEY, L., *The Story of the Sforzas*, 1933.

GARIONI, G. B., *S. Angela Merici*. Queriniana, Brescia, 1950.

Geographical Magazine, March 1958.

GUIDE MOLINARI, *Lac du Garde*. Brescia, 1958.

MAGNAGATI, ALESSANDRO, *La Beata Osanna degli Andreasi*. Padua, 1949.

MARTIN, MOTHER DE SAINT JEAN, O.S.U., *The Spirit of St Angela*. Privately printed, 1950.

MARTINDALE, C. C., *The Vocation of St Aloysius*, 1927.

Miscellanea di Studi Bresciani sull' Alto Medioevo. Brescia, 1959.

New Cambridge Modern History, Vols. I, II.

Ordine et Ceremonie. Brescia, 1545.

PALLUCHIN, RODOLFO, *Carpaccio: Le Storie di Sant' Orsola.* Milan, 1958.

PASTOR, LUDWIG P., *History of the Popes*, Vols. IX, X, XI, 1910–12.

PONNELLE, L., and BORDET, L., *St Philip Neri and the Roman Society of his Times*, 1932.

PRESCOTT, H. F. M., *Jerusalem Journey*, 1954.

Santi dell' Ordine di S. Domenico. Bologna, 1607.

THURSTON, HERBERT, *The Holy Year.* 1950 edition.

UNDSET, SIGRID, *Stages on the Road.* Essay on St Angela Merici, pp. 69–136, 1934.

DATE DUE

DATE DUE			
MAR 15 '74			
APR 11 '74			
NOV 2 9 1976			
FE 22 '79			
NO 7 '82			
DE 1 '83			
JY 26 '85			
NO 19 '86			
AP 30 '87			
OC 4 '87			
DEC 08 '97			
NOV 1 8 '98			
JUL 26 '99			
GAYLORD			PRINTED IN U.S.A.